THE FIRST ARMIES

THE FIRST ARMIES

Doyne Dawson

General Editor: John Keegan

CASSELL&CO

Cassell & Co
Wellington House, 125 Strand
London WC2R 0BB

First published 2001

British Library Cataloguing-in-Publication Data
A catalogue record for this book is available from the
British Library.
ISBN 0-304-35288-8

Cartography: Arcadia Editions
Picture research: Elaine Willis
Special photography: Martin Norris
Design: Martin Hendry

Typeset in Monotype Sabon

Printed and bound in Italy by Printer Trento S.r.l.

ACKNOWLEDGEMENTS

The present volume has profited enormously from the counsel of Robert Drews, who read an early draft of the manuscript and offered invaluable comments and suggestions. I am solely responsible for the conclusions advanced in the final version, and for all errors it may contain. I am grateful to Sir John Keegan, the general editor of the Cassell History of Warfare series, for giving me the opportunity to write this book; and to Penny Gardiner, the project manager, and the rest of the staff at Cassell, for seeing it into print.

DOYNE DAWSON
Seoul, Korea

The Assyrian victory over the Elamites at the Ulai River, 653 BC.

CONTENTS

KEY TO MAPS

General symbols

✕   site of battle

▥   fort or fortified settlement

➤   movement

Geographical symbols

    urban area

    urban area (3D maps)

———   river

– – –   seasonal river

·······   canal

●   town/city

– – –   internal border

———   international border

———   main trade route

■ ■ ■   possible trade route

MAP LIST

CHRONOLOGY

The *Assyrian King List* provides us with a reasonably firm chronology for events in Mesopotamia, and hence for the Middle East in general, from the tenth century BC onwards. Before that the synchronous study of the many different king lists allows us to reconstruct a rough chronology for Mesopotamia back to *c.* 2300 BC, when the Akkadian rulers adopted the practice of naming years after important events, such as military campaigns and building projects. This system persisted until *c.* 1500 BC, when the Kassite kings of Babylon began to date by regnal years (e.g., 'in the third year of king so-and-so'). These lists of year-names and kings are our main sources of information about warfare, especially when the scribes filled in descriptions of major events under each year, thereby turning the lists into 'annals'. This tradition culminated in the great royal annals of Assyria between the ninth and seventh centuries. They can be supplemented by the *Babylonian Chronicle*, a year-by-year account of events affecting southern Mesopotamia from 774 to 668 BC.

Towards the end of our period there is also real narrative history, a genre independently invented by Jews and Greeks. The historical books of the Bible, written probably in the seventh or sixth century on the basis of earlier chronicles and oral traditions, allow us a look at the Assyrian Empire from the perspective of one of its client states. The *Histories* of Herodotus, who visited Babylon and collected traditions going back to late Assyrian times, give us a notion of what Mesopotamians of the fifth century thought about their past.

For Egypt, there is a more or less reliable relative chronology to *c.* 2900 BC, owing to the preservation of a complete king list including all the pharaohs back to the First Dynasty. In the third century BC an Egyptian priest named Manetho wrote in Greek a *History of Egypt*, some of which has been preserved by Christian writers, dividing Egyptian history before the Persian conquest into thirty dynasties; this can be supplemented by fragments of earlier king lists. Egyptian chronology can also be verified by astronomical observations but there is much dispute over the interpretation of this data for dates before the first millennium BC.

In other parts of the Middle East, such as Anatolia and the Levant, events must be dated by correlation with Egyptian and Mesopotamian chronology.

Hence the reader should assume a margin of error of at least a century for all dates in the Bronze Age, or before 1000 BC. The central debate concerns certain observations of the planet Venus recorded in a Babylonian omen text which give us a choice between 'high', 'middle', and 'low' chronologies for the Bronze Age. By the high chronology, the dates of the reign of Hammurabi of Babylon were 1848–1806 BC; by the middle, 1792–1750 BC; by the low, 1728–1686 BC. For the sake of convenience I have generally followed the middle chronology, which is the one used in the most recent edition of *The Cambridge Ancient History*. But readers should be aware that for many events most specialists would currently prefer a different dating. In recent years Egyptologists have tended to favour lower dates than those in *The Cambridge Ancient History* for Egyptian history before 1000 BC; I have therefore adopted the low dates for Egyptian campaigns of the New Kingdom.

EARLY BRONZE AGE

MESOPOTAMIA		EGYPT	
3100–2900*	Late Uruk Period	3100–2686	Early Dynastic Period
2900–2350	Early Dynastic Period	2686–2181	Old Kingdom (Dynasties 3–6)
2371–2191	First Dynasty of Akkad	2181–2040	First Intermediate Period
2113–2006	Third Dynasty of Ur		

MIDDLE BRONZE AGE

MESOPOTAMIA		EGYPT	
c. 2000–1800	Isin-Larsa Period	2040–1786	Middle Kingdom (Dynasties 11–12)
1792–1750	Hammurabi of Babylon	1786–1567	Second Intermediate Period (Hyksos)

LATE (HIGH) BRONZE AGE

MESOPOTAMIA		EGYPT	
1595–1158	Kassite Dynasty of Babylon	1552–1080	New Kingdom (Dynasties 18–20)
c. 1350–1030	Middle Assyrian Kingdom		

IRON AGE

MESOPOTAMIA		EGYPT	
(Neo-) Assyrian Empire – Early Phase		1080–656	Third Intermediate Period
883–859	Ashurnasirpal II		(Dynasties 21–25)
858–824	Shalmaneser III	656–525	Dynasty 26 (Saite)

(Neo-) Assyrian Empire – Late Phase	
744–727	Tiglath-Pileser III
726–722	Shalmaneser V
721–705	Sargon II
704–681	Sennacherib
680–669	Esarhaddon
668–627?	Ashurbanipal

(Neo-) Babylonian Empire	
625–605	Nablopolassar
604–562	Nebuchadrezzar II
555–539	Nabonidus

Note: The precise accession date of an Assyrian king is unknown. The Assyrian calendar named years, which began in the spring, after eponymous year-officials, and the king was normally year-official in the first or second year of his reign; the year in which he became king would be counted as the last year of his predecessor's reign.

*All dates are BC

The Evolution of Warfare to the Sixth Century bc

A New Guinea warrior of the Iwan tribe. New Guinea is an area of unique importance for the anthropology of war because its traditions of tribal warfare fought with stone weapons persisted into the late twentieth century. One of the insights of modern anthropology is that the war patterns of primitive or pre-state peoples differ from those of states, chiefly in that war is not an instrument of conscious political policy. But this implies no Rousseauian myth about peaceful savages. Most primitive tribes are far from peaceable and their warfare is far from innocuous.

THE EVOLUTION OF WARFARE TO THE SIXTH CENTURY BC

Here are statements made by two famous philosophers on the functions of war:

> So that in the nature of man, we find three principal causes of quarrel. First, competition; secondly, diffidence; thirdly, glory. The first maketh men invade for gain; the second, for safety; and the third, for reputation.
>
> Thomas Hobbes, *Leviathan* (1651)

> War is a mere continuation of policy by other means.
>
> Carl von Clausewitz, *On War* (1832)

Hobbes found the roots of war in the nature of man; Clausewitz, in the nature of politics. Clausewitz was thinking of the wars of highly organized bureaucratic states like those of early modern Europe; Hobbes, of warfare as practised by peoples living below the institutional level of the state, like the savages of America. It did not occur to either that there might have been something even below the level of the wars of savages. Now there is reason to think that there was. Hence the first chapter of this volume is about Darwinian warfare, or proto-warfare, and will trace the roots of war into the animal past of mankind. The second chapter deals with Hobbesian warfare, or the warfare of pre-state societies. Chapters three to five cover Clausewitzian warfare – the continuation of primitive warfare with some admixture of politics, to turn Clausewitz's dictum on its head – in its formative stages, in the region now called the Middle East (south-west Eurasia and north-east Africa) from roughly 3500 to 500 BC. (The parallel development of state-level warfare in east Asia after 1500 BC is to be left to Ralph Sawyer's volume in this series: *The Chinese Empire and Warfare*.)

The most influential modern work on military strategy is On War *by the Prussian general Carl von Clausewitz (1780–1831), veteran of the Napoleonic Wars. He defined warfare as simply* Politik *(a German word that means both 'politics' and 'policy') with the admixture of 'other means'.*

The vast time spans and the fragmentary nature of the evidence present problems unlike those normally encountered in military histories. Warfare in the usual sense probably did not begin until some fifty thousand years ago, a late date in human evolution but still ten times as long as the entire span of recorded history. There can of course be no attempt at a 'history' of prehistoric warfare and some would doubt that there can be an anthropology. Most of the present volume is concerned with the pre-classical civilizations, a relatively brief period of three thousand years, but even that is longer than all the rest of recorded history. Furthermore, the history of the earliest Orient is not like the sort of narrative to which most readers of history are accustomed. They may feel numbed by the seemingly endless lists of dynasties and kings with unpronounceable names in a bewildering variety of dead languages and scripts, and until biblical times are reached it is almost never possible to flesh out the bare account into what is normally expected of an historical narrative. Until we reach the first millennium BC even basic chronology is uncertain; all earlier dates have margins of error of a century or more. The history of war is particularly opaque. We shall always know relatively little about pre-classical warfare. The Greco-Roman tradition of writing narrative history did not exist, except among the Hebrews late in our period, and even Hebrew historical writing never developed any interest in realistic military narrative. In only a few cases can any attempt be made to reconstruct the course of a battle, and the difficulties attending such attempts will be obvious in what follows. Archaeology can tell us much about arms and armour, for some periods more than others, but never about the use of the weapons, which is where the real problem lies.

A stylized confrontation of warriors on a bronze pectoral from north Italy, sixth century BC. European chiefdoms of the early Iron Age were on or near the threshold of the state and represent a transition between tribal warfare and the Clausewitzian wars of policy.

I suggest that pre-classical military history has been further obscured by the assumption that the nature and functions of warfare have not basically changed since civilization began. Land warfare between civilized states, from the time it entered the light of history in the first millennium BC, has been essentially infantry warfare; cavalry has always played a subsidiary role on the battlefield, sometimes abetted by other subsidiary arms such as chariots and elephants. Among some nomadic peoples, especially on the Eurasian steppes, there has flourished a quite different military tradition, based on cavalry; we will encounter some of its representatives in the final chapter of this volume. But the wars of complex agrarian societies seem always to turn on the clash of masses of foot soldiers in more or less disciplined formations. It is hence commonly,

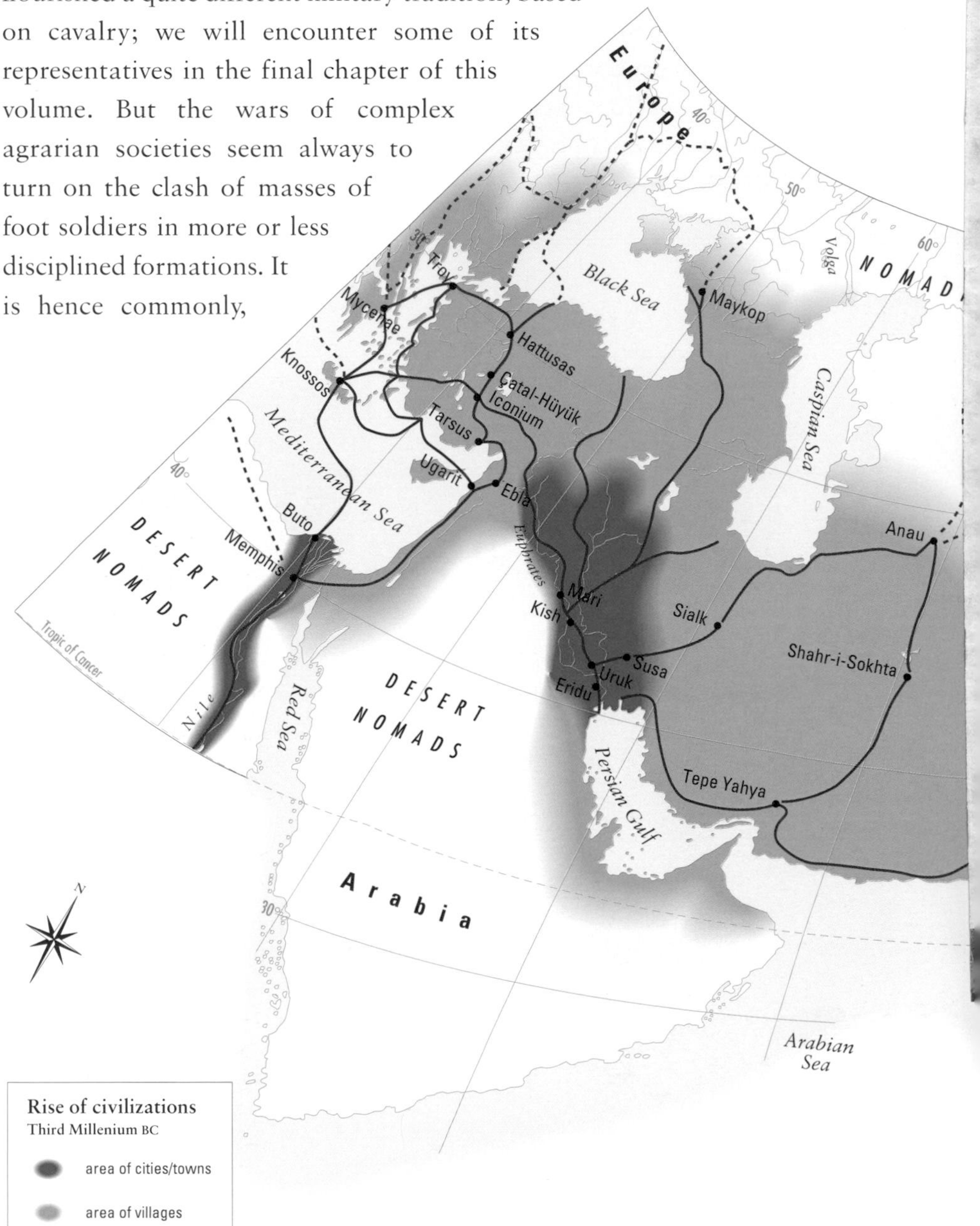

Rise of civilizations
Third Millenium BC

area of cities/towns

area of villages

• early urban centre

main trade route of the settled zone

- - - route to pastoral/nomadic zones

and not unreasonably assumed that state-level warfare of the Clausewitzian type must have arisen simultaneously with the rise of the state in about 3000 BC, and that infantry warfare arose at the same time.

But it will be argued herein that in fact there was a startling time gap, two thousand years long, between the rise of the state and the rise of state-level warfare. Three stages can be discerned in that long transition. Clausewitzian warfare became technically possible with the development of city states in Mesopotamia by 3000 BC, but the evidence suggests that did not happen. Instead the first states poured their resources into fortification, a purely defensive strategy which prohibited offensive warfare; insofar as offensive warfare existed, it was probably little different from that of the Stone Age, and no more effective as an instrument for achieving political objectives. In the second stage, after 1700 BC, offensive wars between well-organized states became common, but this was a type of warfare unlike any before or since, relying upon élite groups of horsed chariotry, with such infantry as there was in a passive and subsidiary role. Finally, after 1000 BC, the first true infantry formations appeared, as did the first true cavalry, and the art of war as we know it was born.

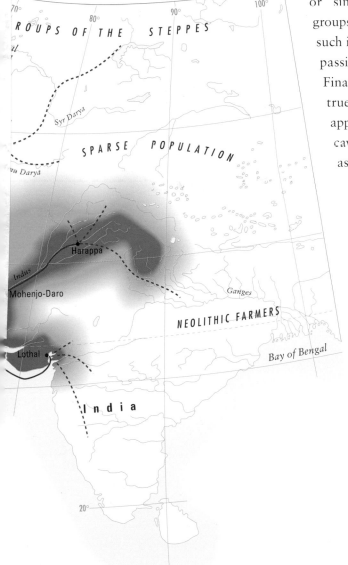

THE RISE OF CIVILIZATIONS, THIRD MILLENNIUM BC

This map shows the geographical environment of the earliest civilizations. All grew up on the alluvial plains of great rivers adjacent to the highlands where agriculture was born. Literate urban cultures and centralized states appeared in the Tigris–Euphrates basin c. 3500 BC, on the Nile c. 3200 BC, and on the Indus c. 2500 BC. In the second millennium BC a fourth civilization arose on the Yellow River in China (off the map).

CHAPTER ONE

THE ROOTS
OF WAR

CHIMPANZEES ROUTINELY HUNT small animals. Male chimps account for 90 per cent of the kills, and almost all the kills of larger game such as monkeys. Females receive meat from males, who share it with other band members to ensure social and sexual dominance. In addition parties of adult males patrol the borders of their territory, attacking trespassers from neighbouring bands, and may stealthily intrude into the neighbouring territory. On these raids solitary 'foreign' chimps are ambushed and killed, but females in heat are likely to be adopted.

THE ROOTS OF WAR

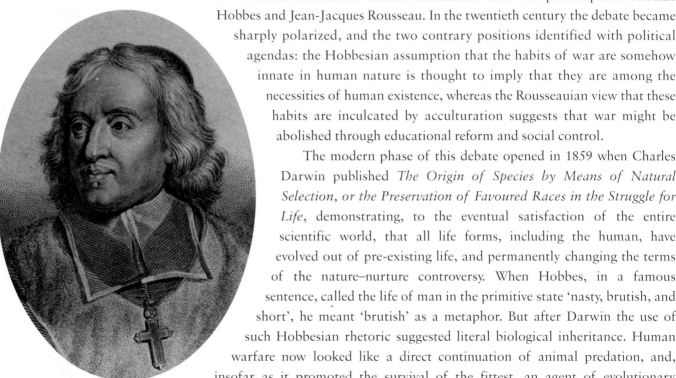

The Leviathan *of the English philosopher Thomas Hobbes (1588–1679) described the state of nature as a 'State of Warre' where human life was 'solitary, poor, nasty, brutish, and short.' From the Greek historian Thucydides Hobbes took the idea that war is rooted in innate drives for gain, safety, and glory.*

THE NATURE OF THE PROBLEM

Military histories rarely devote much space to discussing the causes of war, as this subject is assumed to belong to some discipline other than history. But there is no agreement as to which one. Debate over the causes of war has long focused on the question of whether warfare is a product of nature or nurture, inheritance or environment, a subject for the natural sciences or the social sciences. This controversy has sputtered on inconclusively since the Enlightenment, when the two alternatives received classic formulation from the philosophers Thomas Hobbes and Jean-Jacques Rousseau. In the twentieth century the debate became sharply polarized, and the two contrary positions identified with political agendas: the Hobbesian assumption that the habits of war are somehow innate in human nature is thought to imply that they are among the necessities of human existence, whereas the Rousseauian view that these habits are inculcated by acculturation suggests that war might be abolished through educational reform and social control.

The modern phase of this debate opened in 1859 when Charles Darwin published *The Origin of Species by Means of Natural Selection, or the Preservation of Favoured Races in the Struggle for Life*, demonstrating, to the eventual satisfaction of the entire scientific world, that all life forms, including the human, have evolved out of pre-existing life, and permanently changing the terms of the nature–nurture controversy. When Hobbes, in a famous sentence, called the life of man in the primitive state 'nasty, brutish, and short', he meant 'brutish' as a metaphor. But after Darwin the use of such Hobbesian rhetoric suggested literal biological inheritance. Human warfare now looked like a direct continuation of animal predation, and, insofar as it promoted the survival of the fittest, an agent of evolutionary progress. 'Social Darwinism' – the application of Darwinian evolutionary logic to human history – was a common trend in the late nineteenth and early twentieth centuries. Nowadays we are often told that this was a perversion of Darwinism, and the ideology of militarists and jingoists. But if we mean simply the assumption that human society has evolved by much the same processes as other animal societies, then Darwin was himself a social Darwinist. The metaphors of struggle that filled the writings of Darwinists did not necessarily imply violent struggle, and social Darwinism could promote either war or peace, depending on which aspect of animal society writers chose to emphasize.

Nevertheless a profound reaction against both Hobbesianism and social Darwinism set in at around the time of the First World War, which dampened the expectation that any kind of struggle could be progressive. Throughout the twentieth century the social and behavioural sciences have leaned towards extreme Rousseauism, and their research has been dominated by a set of assumptions often called 'the standard social science model' (SSSM). This model, which goes back to the founders of modern anthropology such as Émile Durkheim and Franz Boas, assumes that 'culture', a term understood to comprise all organized mental activity, is an autonomous and uniquely human phenomenon, unconnected to the natural world, free of biological and psychological laws, and entirely the product of acculturation. This was widely thought to imply that human nature is a kind of tabula rasa on which practically anything might be written by whichever educators wield the chalk, and that we are free to choose whatever morals, values and other cultural norms we please.

The pervasiveness of this model in twentieth-century educational systems is due largely to the utopian dreams of human perfectibility that it encourages in pacifists, feminists, progressive educators and every sort of radical reformer. To believers in the model it seems obvious that warfare is simply a bad habit resulting from improper education. The title of a 1940 article by Margaret Mead, Boas's disciple and one of the most influential apostles of the SSSM, read 'Warfare is Only an Invention, Not a Biological Necessity'. Social scientists realized the habit was oddly hard to break (this realization was particularly inescapable in the year 1940), but they rarely showed any interest in exploring its roots.

These assumptions were put into a sort of canonical form in the 1986 Seville Statement on Violence issued by an international conference of scientists to celebrate the International Year of Peace proclaimed by the United Nations. This was intended as a counterpart to the UNESCO

The Swiss-born French author Jean-Jacques Rousseau (1712–78), father of Romanticism, popularized the cult of simplicity and nature. His more extreme followers idealized noble savages, perceived human nature as innately peaceable, and blamed warfare on the policies of states.

Statement on Race, and was soon endorsed by the American Anthropological Association and the American Psychological Association. The Seville scientists declared it 'scientifically incorrect to say that we have inherited a tendency to make war from our animal ancestors' or 'that war or any other violent behaviour is genetically programmed into our human nature' or 'that in the course of human evolution there has been a selection for aggressive behaviour'; they affirmed that 'biology does not condemn humanity to war' and anathematized the 'alleged biological findings that have been used ... to justify violence and war'.

By 'alleged biological findings' they meant the revival of social Darwinism. By the 1980s new developments in evolutionary theory, especially in the emerging field of evolutionary psychology, were unexpectedly supporting

ON

THE ORIGIN OF SPECIES

BY MEANS OF NATURAL SELECTION,

OR THE

PRESERVATION OF FAVOURED RACES IN THE STRUGGLE
FOR LIFE.

By CHARLES DARWIN, M.A.,
FELLOW OF THE ROYAL, GEOLOGICAL, LINNÆAN, ETC., SOCIETIES;
AUTHOR OF 'JOURNAL OF RESEARCHES DURING H. M. S. BEAGLE'S VOYAGE
ROUND THE WORLD.'

LONDON:
JOHN MURRAY, ALBEMARLE STREET.
1859.
P. D. B.

The right of Translation is reserved.

'Thus, from the war of nature, from famine and death, the most exalted object which we are capable of conceiving, namely, the production of the higher animals, directly follows ... from so simple a beginning endless forms most beautiful and most wonderful have been, and are being, evolved.' (Charles Darwin)

Hobbes. Evolution had always been something of a problem for the SSSM. That model divided the mind into two categories labelled 'biological' and 'cultural', and assigned all complex social behaviour to the latter; the mind was thus conceived as a general all-purpose reasoning faculty, empty of content until its environment should fill it with information. All these scientists accepted Darwinian evolution, yet none could convincingly explain how a mind like the one described could possibly have evolved on this earth. Therefore evolutionary psychologists, building upon a suggestion made by Darwin at the conclusion of *The Origin of Species*, have proposed a different model: the mind as a network of specialized computer programs that evolved to handle specific adaptive problems such as sharing food, finding mates, parenting, acquiring a language, responding to threats. These mechanisms are thought to be both biological and cultural; they remain latent until called forth by specific cues, so they appear in some societies but not others, and at some periods but not others. If warfare is rooted in such a psychological mechanism, then it is wrong to think of war as genetically programmed, as the Seville scientists feared. Rather, what is genetically programmed is a mechanism that decides which strategy, war or peace, to adopt in the face of threat.

This model may explain the combination of endemic warlikeness and endemic peaceability that make up human history, and the human capacity for lightning changes from one mode to the other. Warlike primitives seem to civilized observers innately ferocious and untamable, but in fact they were domesticated so easily under the pressure of civilization that genuinely primitive warfare has already almost disappeared from the earth. Complex societies can abandon deeply ingrained traditions of militarism just as readily under the pressure of events, as witness the transformation of Germany and Japan after the Second World War. Any explanation of the causes of warfare must account for both its ubiquity and its flexibility, and until a better theory appears neo-Darwinism seems the most plausible approach. There has been a selection for aggressive behaviour in human evolution, but it has not condemned us to either war or peace. The habits of war have imbued the human biological/cultural constitution, but they are not deterministic. That constitution has so evolved that it has no deterministic patterns other than the sort which make babies suckle, cry, crawl and walk.

Many civilized and sophisticated people, who understand that 'determinism' is a false issue, are still deeply reluctant to give up the standard social science model because of the utopian hopes for changing the world that it seems to hold out. If warfare is only a cultural invention, without deeper roots in human nature, then may it not be altogether abolished and forgotten? Unfortunately, that does not follow. During the Cold War it was often and correctly pointed out that nuclear weapons can never be 'disinvented'. They might be suppressed, as the Tokugawa Shogunate suppressed gunpowder in seventeenth-century Japan. But after the last intercontinental ballistic missile has been dismantled the technology that built it will not be forgotten, and others can always be built, unless we are willing to pay the price of giving up post-industrial technology. Likewise warfare might be suppressed, but even if it were only an invention of the state its possibilities would never be forgotten for as long as states exist, and the control of it would still require ceaseless vigilance. If we accept the fact that warfare is in the nature of man, the only difference it makes is that we might then achieve a clearer understanding of the world, which is preferable to a delusory and hubristic hope of changing it, and entertain more realistic expectations of controlling the mechanisms of war.

ANTS AND APES

Let us define our subject. Warfare is *coalitional intraspecific aggression*. It is a form of agonistic behaviour that involves organized and lethal conflicts between two groups of the same species. It is not to be confused with aggression per se, which is everywhere in the animal world, and too generalized a concept to be useful; nor with interspecific predation and competition, for only in folklore are different species said to make war on each other; nor with the violent and often lethal combats that occur between individuals of the same species, especially between individual males for access to females. There is a connection between the last phenomenon and human warfare, which tends to be an all-male business, but normal male rivalry over females is by definition an individualistic matter which does not lend itself easily to coalitional behaviour.

Genuinely coalitional aggression is very rare in the animal world. It seems to have evolved only twice, once in the line of primates that has ended in ourselves, and before that among the ants. (Actually it must have evolved independently many times among the ten thousand species of ants, but this was probably replication of the same basic process.) It is rare because co-operative behaviour is normally restricted to kinship groups. In current Darwinian theory, evolution takes place through 'inclusive fitness', which means that natural selection operates so as to encourage behavioural strategies that enhance the survival and reproduction of individuals and their close relatives, who share much the same genotype. This condition places a strict limitation on the size of co-operative groups, and only the social insects have broken that barrier by creating closely related kin groups of enormous size. A tropical anthill may contain 20 million ants, but all except one are siblings, and the colony behaves and evolves like a single organism.

In the ant world, all-out combat between two neighbouring communities for territory, food stores and slaves, often ending in the extinction of one of them, is so common that it seems a forced move in the game of evolutionary design; and the analogies in human society are close enough that one is tempted to call this a case of convergent evolution. But we find these analogies only at a late date in human history. Humans did not practise the ant kind of warfare until they lived in communities that resemble anthills – sedentary, densely populated, rigorously organized, highly territorial. Such human anthills did not appear until the rise of the first agrarian civilizations five thousand years ago, and it will be argued later

This Australian anthill may contain many millions of inhabitants, a larger population than many of the kingdoms of men, yet it behaves like a single great animal. Ant colonies may be described as super-organisms. Virtually immune from predators, their only enemies are other ants; hence the prevalence of intraspecific warfare.

that even after such societies arose it was many centuries before they began to wage offensive territorial wars against one another. We came to this late, and came to it reluctantly and timidly, compared to the fierce solidarity and ruthlessness of ants. Therefore insect evolution is of no help in trying to explain the uniquely human type of coalitional aggression in its earlier stages.

To explain that we must look at the animals around us, not those down at our feet. We may suppose, for reasons to be considered shortly, that early

Among ants that live in large colonies deadly internecine warfare is extremely common between neighbouring communities of the same or related species.

mankind, during the formative stages of human society, lived by hunting big game in an open plains environment. The social carnivores that inhabit a comparable ecological niche today – lion (*Panthera leo*), spotted hyena (*Crocuta crocuta*), African wild dog (*Lycaon pictus*) and wolf (*Canis lupus*) – all engage in intraspecific combats, occasionally lethal, between neighbouring packs or prides in defence of their territories. These fights are not truly coalitional, as these species lack the necessary degree of social intelligence. But it seems significant that social predators will so readily turn the habits of co-operative hunting to co-operative defence against their own kind. Lions, hyenas and wild

A pride of lions working in concert can kill game as large as a hippopotamus (shown here) or a half-grown elephant. Until the appearance of advanced hominids the social carnivores had no natural enemies. Animals at the top of the food chain, like ants, lions, and men, compete only with their own kind.

dogs were the chief competitors of hominids on the African plains through the whole course of hominid evolution, until the point about ten thousand years ago when mankind was compelled to give up the hunting life, and in the African game parks their remnant populations still hunt; but the wolf, northern counterpart of the wild dog, entered at that point into a symbiotic relationship with man that promised its genes a larger future.

Early researchers on human origins paid more attention to the social carnivores than to the great apes, our closest living relatives, because the apes were believed to be strict vegetarians and early man was believed to be a

OVERLEAF: *A pack of wild dogs brings down a wildebeest. Among mammalian carnivores the African wild dog represents the apex of social co-operation. Within the pack mating is restricted to the dominant pair, whose pups are cared for by all their packmates.*

specialized big-game hunter from far back. When they looked to primates they focused on the baboon, the only large primate other than man that ever adapted completely to life on the treeless plains. It was found that these big fierce monkeys had a high degree of social complexity, as animals tend to have in that menacing environment; that they carry out considerable small-game hunting, of fawns and hares and the like, and indeed eat more flesh than any other primate but man, for a tropical savannah is the most game-rich environment on earth and highly conducive to carnivorous habits; and that their bands, often more than a hundred strong, engage in intraspecific conflicts with neighbouring troops which produce appalling noise levels and some bloodshed. Beyond that the observation of baboons added little to the information gleaned from the plains carnivores.

The discovery of the real chimpanzee was a different matter. In the 1970s the anthropologist Jane Goodall found that the common chimpanzee (*Pan troglodytes*) is not the peaceful vegetarian it had been thought. Chimpanzee bands routinely practise co-operative hunting of monkeys and other small animals, and also conduct lethal raids into the territories of neighbouring chimp bands. These conflicts differ from the intraspecific conflicts described above in that the fighting, like the hunting, is primarily the work of male chimpanzees, whereas in other species the females are at least as active as the males in group defence; and among chimps both hunting and fighting seem to show a degree of planning and orchestration. In other words, there is something eerily human about the business. This drew attention because by this time molecular analysis had revealed that humans and chimpanzees are genetically much closer than was thought. They are descended from a common ancestor that lived only 5 to 8 million years ago.

What is there about chimpanzees that could give rise to such a special pattern of agonistic behaviour? Three factors have been pointed out. Firstly, there is a peculiar social organization. Chimpanzees are one of the few primates in which males stay in their natal group after adolescence and females leave it. Most primate societies are essentially bands of related females with their attached males, but a chimp society is a band of related males with their attached females. They are mildly polygynous and there is a ranking order among males, but little mating competition and no lethal combats. The sexual dimorphism of chimpanzees is moderate, with males averaging 125 per cent larger than females, just as in humans. Gorillas and orangutans, by contrast, are highly polygynous, and males fight savagely over females, who are less than half their size, extreme sexual dimorphism being a sign of extreme polygyny in all mammals. In most mammalian species it pays in terms of inclusive fitness for males to fight one another for dominance and access to females; but in a species with male-retentive groups it pays for males to co-operate with one another and compete as a group with other brotherhoods to defend their territory and females.

The male gorilla (right) is twice the size of the female. The sexual dimorphism of chimpanzees is comparatively slight, a factor favouring co-operation rather than competition between males. But the australopithecines were more dimorphic, which may indicate some reversion to polygyny.

At least it pays if the rewards of coalitional behaviour are worth fighting for. For there also seems to be an ecological factor at work. Another surprising outcome of recent research is that the other chimpanzee species, the relatively little-known pygmy chimpanzee or bonobo (*Pan paniscus*), does not practise co-operative hunting or intraspecific conflict, or at least not to nearly the same degree as its larger cousin, and intraspecific killing has never been observed. The two animals are very closely related; *P. paniscus* was only recently recognized as a distinct species. The most plausible explanation of the difference in behaviour is that the pygmy chimp lives in a food-rich habitat and does not have to forage in small parties like the common chimp. Small groups scattered through the forest are vulnerable to raid and reprisal.

Finally, most importantly, a certain level of social intelligence is required. The great apes, and especially the chimpanzees, are said to be the only creatures other than ourselves that display 'Machiavellian intelligence'. They can imagine what other animals are thinking and can attribute intentions to them; they can picture other possible worlds and design alternative scenarios; they can

empathize; they can practise deception and cruelty. Only that sort of social cognition makes possible genuine coalitional behaviour, for an effective coalition cannot be forged without the ability to assess the capacities and loyalties of its members. There are a few species of monkey that have male-retentive social organization but they do not form lasting male affiliations like chimps because they lack that kind of intelligence.

Much of what has been said about chimpanzees applies also to the most primitive human societies, those living at the hunting-and-gathering level of culture, of which the Australian aborigines before contact with Europeans may represent the purest example. All hunting-and-gathering cultures are by definition foragers, and must travel long distances in small parties in search of foods that are hard to find. In all those known to anthropology, hunting and warfare are essentially male activities – *the* essentially male activities – and, in all, male bonding is a central institution while bonding between females is relatively weak and socially insignificant, except when women are united by attachment to the same man. The great majority of these cultures are patrilocal,

The pygmy chimpanzee or bonobo inhabits a restricted range in the Congo rainforest. There has been little observation in the wild, but the available evidence suggests it is strikingly different from the common chimp in social behaviour, with little male dominance, hunting, or intraspecific violence, and no tool use.

an anthropological term meaning that males stay in the natal group after adolescence and females leave it to marry into other groups. (It might be pointed out that this arrangement is not necessary to male bonding among humans as it is among apes, because humans have language and can form lasting affiliations with either gender regardless of genealogical relationships or spatial proximity. The 20 per cent of known hunter-gatherers who are matrilocal are just as male-bonded as the patrilocal cultures. But the preference for patrilocality still seems significant.) And the native Australians of course possessed a potential Machiavellian intelligence on the level of Machiavelli, not that of a chimpanzee.

A plausible portrait of the common ancestor of 5 million years ago can be reconstructed. It was probably a cunning ape that lived in closed, stable, male-retentive social groups and had strong tendencies to male-coalitional behaviour, especially when expressing hostility to outsiders. In those tendencies can be found the ultimate roots of warfare.

The biologist Edward O. Wilson, a specialist in the study of ants and a pioneer in the application of evolutionary science to human behaviour, put forward the following conjectures on the origins of what anthropologists have called 'ethnocentricity', by which is meant the human tendency to form exclusive groups:

> Human beings are strongly predisposed to respond with unreasoning hatred to external threats and to escalate their hostility sufficiently to overwhelm the sources of the threat by a sufficiently wide margin of safety. Our brains do appear to be programmed to the following extent: we are inclined to partition other people into friends and aliens, in the same sense that birds are inclined to learn territorial songs and to navigate by the polar constellations. We tend to fear deeply the actions of strangers and to solve conflicts by aggression. These learning rules are most likely to have evolved during the past hundreds of thousands of years of human evolution and, thus, to have conferred a biological advantage on those who conformed to them with the greatest fidelity.
>
> *On Human Nature* (1978)

More recent work in evolutionary science suggests that these learning rules may have evolved over millions of years.

The hypothesis that the real cause of warfare is ethnocentricity has serious implications. It means that warfare is an expression of the human capacity for co-operativeness and fraternity, not egoism and competitiveness. Xenophobia is the other side of ethnocentrism, warlikeness the other side of peaceability; in-group amity requires out-group enmity. What is missing from Hobbes's analysis is the coalition. It is indeed in the nature of man to invade for safety, gain and glory, but he does this for his group, not for himself.

Another implication of the neo-Darwinian hypothesis is that proto-ethnocentricity and proto-xenophobia, such as it attributes to the common ancestor and by implication to the earliest hominids, were products of sexual selection. It has been mentioned that among mammals sexual selection tends to produce violent conflict between males. Males compete for females, not the other way around, because to males mating costs nothing and it pays reproductively to have access to as many females as possible, whereas females rarely need access to males and there is no reproductive point in fighting over them. From the point of view of the male genes, even extremely high-risk strategies can pay. Mammalian sexual aggression is male against male, but under the right circumstances, such as the scenario outlined above, there seems no reason why patterns of intercoalitional violence should not evolve. It seems likely that one has. The wars of ants are fought by females, but if a mammal did anything of that sort it would almost certainly be a male affair.

BECOMING HUMAN

The first fossils of *Australopithecus* were discovered in 1924, but not until the 1960s was it generally accepted as the long-sought 'missing link' between ape and human. Since then a fairly clear picture of human origins has taken shape, though the details are fuzzy, and new discoveries change the picture constantly. Only its outlines will be sketched here.

In the Miocene epoch, which began 25 million years ago, the earth was warm and wet, and in the dense forests that blanketed Africa flourished many kinds of apes, one of them the common ancestor. With the coming of the Pliocene, 5 million years ago, a cooling and drying trend set in, and forests gave way to grasslands. The apes, except for one species, retreated before the more adaptable monkeys and eventually became confined to their present remnant populations in the diminished equatorial rainforest belt. On the spreading savannahs appeared many new animals adapted to life in the open, including the fast modern antelopes and equids, and the efficient socialized carnivores like lions and hyenas. There was also a new kind of primate that went on two legs.

These australopithecine primates were not prepossessing in appearance. They resembled slightly built chimpanzees, weighing about 90 pounds, with brains only slightly larger than a chimp's. Their main evolutionary novelty was a primitive form of bipedalism, and there has been much debate over the reasons for that unique adaptation. Ever since Darwin it had been thought that hominids became bipedal to use tools, but the discovery of the australopithecines disproved that, for there is no reason to credit them with any tool-using capacity much more impressive than that of a chimpanzee. It seems clearly an adaptation to a semi-terrestrial existence and was probably the result

Australopithecines were once envisioned as big-game hunters on the open plains, but now it is thought they rarely moved far from trees, foraging for plants and small animals in the same way that chimps do, perhaps also scavenging; the sabre-toothed cats, which preyed on elephants and other megafauna, must have left many huge carcasses about.

37

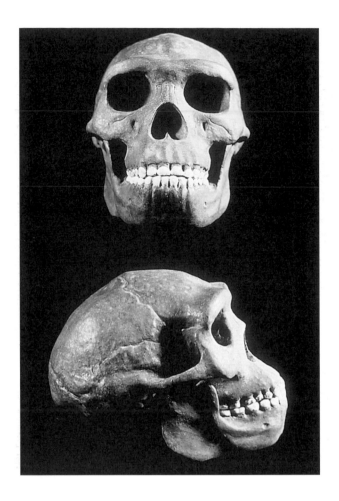

Homo erectus, *discovered in the Far East in 1891 and at first called 'Peking Man' and 'Java Man,' was probably the first true human. Some palaeoanthropologists would divide* H. erectus *into several species, but they were all very similar and may be collectively referred to as the 'erectines'.*

of a habitat change from true forest to open country. A monkey that leaves the trees will become quadrupedal, like the baboon; but an ape, for anatomical reasons, has a choice between bipedalism and walking on the knuckles like a gorilla, so bipedalism may have been the best option available. It had the side effect of freeing the hands for carrying things, such as food, infants and tools, and so opened the way for more dramatic adaptations, but to judge from the fossil record it was a very long time before any such opportunities were exploited. There is no reason to attribute to australopithecines anything but apelike social behaviour, except perhaps their success. The various australopithecine species (some seven are now recognized) flourished for 2 million years across a huge stretch of Africa from Ethiopia to the Cape, in an environment filled with alarming predators; yet they were smaller and weaker than the great apes, had no natural weapons like the formidable fangs of the baboons, and would have been easy to catch on the ground. They certainly retained considerable tree-climbing ability (their favoured habitat seems to have been wooded savannah), but also must have been capable of co-ordinated defence, perhaps with some improvement on the chimpanzee's ability to wield sticks and stones as weapons, both for defence and for hunting.

The first artificial tools appeared in the late Pliocene, 2.5 million years ago. These are crudely chipped stone hand-axes, but the piles of bones found with them leave no doubt they were used to butcher large animals. The hominids appear to have scavenged carcasses left by predators such as sabre-toothed cats, and dragged the meat to butchering sites. Natural selection had begun to select for intelligence and tool-using ability.

At the beginning of the Pleistocene or Ice Age, 1.8 million years ago, the African plains became arid and treeless, and over them roamed *Homo erectus*, perhaps the first hominid we would recognize as 'human' if we met them. They were fully bipedal, as tall as many modern humans, with brains two-thirds the size of ours. They quickly became the dominant species in Africa and then spread over most of the Old World. They could use fire and had a much-improved stone tool kit, and though the point was long disputed there is now no doubt they hunted big game. In a German bog were recently found several long, well-balanced sprucewood throwing spears made 400,000 years ago, and a Spanish site of around that time has yielded the butchered remains of thirty elephants, perhaps driven into a swamp with fire. But we do not know to what extent their way of life deviated from the chimpanzee pattern. It is possible they thought like intelligent apes.

The erectine hominid was a supremely successful animal, who was lord of the world for 1.5 million years. But 200,000 years ago they began to be squeezed out by brainier types of hominid. In the northern parts of the Old World they were replaced by the big-brained, big-bodied *Homo neanderthalensis*, whom some consider a subspecies of *Homo sapiens*. In southern parts, anatomically modern humans, *Homo sapiens*, emerged 100,000 years ago and 40,000 years ago had spread over the entire Old World, in the process replacing all other hominid types, though how remains open to conjecture.

The more important facts presented in the above outline would probably not be seriously questioned except by biblical fundamentalists, but it has said nothing much about the way hominids become human. What do we mean by 'human'? In terms of social organization, the most obvious factor that unmistakably distinguishes every primitive human group from every group of non-human primates is the sexual division of labour: men hunt and women gather, and food is shared at a home base. Women may gather grubs and trap small animals, and the whole tribe may join in driving a herd over a cliff, but stalking and killing big game is under all normal circumstances an exclusively male occupation in all the known hunting-and-gathering cultures. The division of labour requires a home base. Apes do not have bases and do not share food, though they tolerate scrounging, and a male chimpanzee that has made a kill may give meat to a female in exchange for sexual favours. Division of labour and genuine food sharing imply the existence of the peculiar human family structure, in which males as well as females invest in parenting, a thing utterly unknown in other primates. The key factor in the systematic development of human family and band structure may have been the rise of intensive big-game hunting, which made available great quantities of meat on an irregular basis, and made food sharing highly adaptive. A hunting-and-gathering group organized in that way was a superbly well-adapted social organism, living at the top of the food chain, immune from predators, with no rivals except groups like itself.

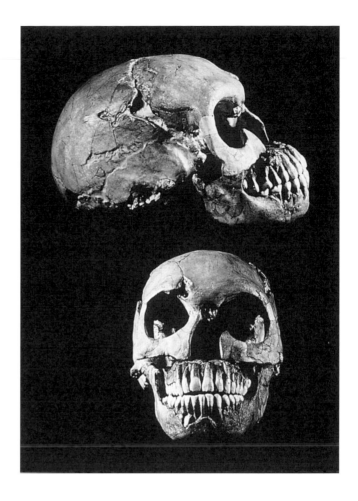

Neanderthal man was the earliest fossil human discovered and remains the best documented. By 125,000 years ago, during the last interglacial (warm period in the Ice Age), they had spread all over Europe and the Middle East. Their brains were larger than ours but it is doubtful they were capable of real language.

The Clacton spearpoint, made 300,000 years ago, is one of the oldest weapons known. In Germany in 1948 a complete spear 125,000 years old was found embedded between the ribs of an elephant. Recently even older spears have been found. But none have stone heads.

Artist's conception of men – perhaps made to look too modern – hunting fallow deer in England 200,000 years ago. These fossils, found at Swanscombe in the 1930s, are classified as Homo heidelbergensis, *a type of erectine that inhabited Europe from 700,000 years ago and may have been the ancestor of the Neanderthals.*

Every aspect of this system obviously needed high social intelligence and probably required some kind of language. But we do not know when such humans appeared. Erectines did some big-game hunting, Neanderthals did it intensively, but it has been questioned whether either was capable of grammatical language. No one doubts that even the earliest *H. sapiens*, being anatomically indistinguishable from ourselves, was physically capable of such language, and it is difficult to believe they did not have a recognizably human culture of the type described above, but it has left little sign of itself. Between the first evidence for anatomically modern humans and the first evidence for mentally, spiritually, culturally modern humans there is a gap of 60,000 years.

THE CULTURAL EXPLOSION

According to evolutionary psychologists, the human mind evolved by developing specialized programmes to solve enduring adaptive problems, mostly having to do with social exchanges. After a certain point in human evolution the only selective pressures on the evolutionary process would have come from other human groups, producing a cognitive arms race that spurred further breakthroughs in Machiavellian social intelligence. At a further point the domain-specific programmes of the hominid mind linked up to form the kind of consciousness the reader possesses – a general reasoning faculty; these disembodied minds then linked up to form a disembodied 'culture' in the standard social science sense, though a culture with more biological ties than that model supposes. The creation of a fully human awareness meant the start of an entirely new kind of evolutionary process. Biological evolution is dependent on kinship, and there are strict limits on the size of co-operative groups unless they can reproduce like ants. There are no limits to the size of the reciprocal social networks produced by disembodied culture, and it can pursue fitness goals with fantastic speed, compared to the glacial processes of genetic evolution.

Such minds have not left clear signs in the archaeological record until 40,000–50,000 years ago – the birth of the Upper Palaeolithic culture, the climax of the Old Stone Age. The most obvious change is the flowering of visual arts. Before then it is hard to find any human artefact that can be described as an art object. Everything made by erectines and Neanderthals, and almost everything made by anatomically modern people for their first 60,000 years was strictly functional, though claims have been made for isolated 'art objects' from far back. But in the Upper Palaeolithic all manufactured objects containing any space large enough are likely to be carved, painted or otherwise decorated. With the birth of art came the birth of style. Other species are practically uniform in social behaviour, and to judge from the monotonous uniformity of the artefact record so were hominids until the Upper Palaeolithic, but after that every locality stamps everything it makes with its own assertive, emblematic, self-

The climax of Upper Palaeolithic art was the Magdalenian culture, which appeared in France 18,000 years ago, at the coldest point of the last glaciation. The Magdalenian artists produced the famous cave paintings and many superb sculptures like this bison carved from bone.

Modern humans originated in Africa and arrived in Europe 40,000 years ago. Soon after appeared the Aurignacian culture, which produced the first unequivocal art objects. This carved mammoth tusk from Moravia is dated 25,000 to 30,000 years old. The earliest calendars and musical instruments belong to the same time.

The oldest and simplest tools are those of the Oldowan tradition, 2.5–1.5 million years ago, often pebbles with one end chipped off (right). They were replaced by the flaked Acheulean style, which was associated with erectines (centre and left, Acheulean hand axes, 1 million and 350,000 years old).

identifying forms and techniques. The crude weapons of the earlier Stone Age are replaced by beautifully shaped blades in a variety of standardized forms. Evidence of structured imagination is everywhere. At the same time the colonization of the Australasian islands and the American Arctic gives evidence not only of high population density (by a hunter's standards) across the Old World but also of levels of information exchange, planning, and social/technical expertise capable of exploring highly daunting oceanic and tundra environments.

In short, there is no doubt that a fully human culture existed by the Upper Palaeolithic, and there is hardly more reason to doubt that warfare of the fully human type was already an integral part of it. It is very likely that the remote ancestors of mankind had some innate tendency to proto-ethnocentric

RIGHT: *Compare the Acheulean manufactures (left) with these Upper Palaeolithic spearheads carved from bone, found in Austria. Tools and weapons were for the first time made from materials other than stone, including bone, antler, and horn. Beads and other personal ornaments also appeared.*

behaviour by small kin groups. When culture emerged, cultures built upon this tendency and extended it to all people identified by the same ethnic markers, using cultural ties as replacements for the ties of kinship, forging themselves more or less consciously into adaptive units for the sake of competing with neighbouring cultural groups. It is not necessary to assume there was any innate tendency behind this, and those determined to believe that warfare is a purely 'cultural invention' are free to ignore this suggestion. But if we do not, it then becomes easier to understand the universality of the institution, its association with masculinity and its animal analogues.

Probably we should imagine a long and gradual transition from an apelike pattern of lethal male raiding, in which individuals from neighbouring bands may be stalked and murdered, but without any organized combat between coalitions, to the fully developed institution of 'primitive warfare' to be examined in the next chapter. It is possible that some kind of incipient warfare, with incipient division of labour and incipient fatherhood, existed even among the erectines. But the immense time lag between the physical emergence of modern man and his cultural efflorescence suggests a long period of maturation. Warfare seems dependent upon what the psychologist Erik Erikson called 'pseudospeciation', the process of differentiation by which human groups come to perceive one another as if they were totally different species and treat one another accordingly. It seems doubtful that such a degree of cultural differentiation was reached before the Upper Palaeolithic. The wide dispersal of hunting cultures, which may occupy territories a hundred miles across, must have long hindered cultural exchanges both in peace and war.

OVERLEAF: *An aboriginal band in the Northern Territory of Australia prepares for an initiation ceremony. Elaborate rituals initiating adolescent boys into manhood are pervasive in the tribal world. In warlike cultures they can take the form of frightening ordeals by torture.*

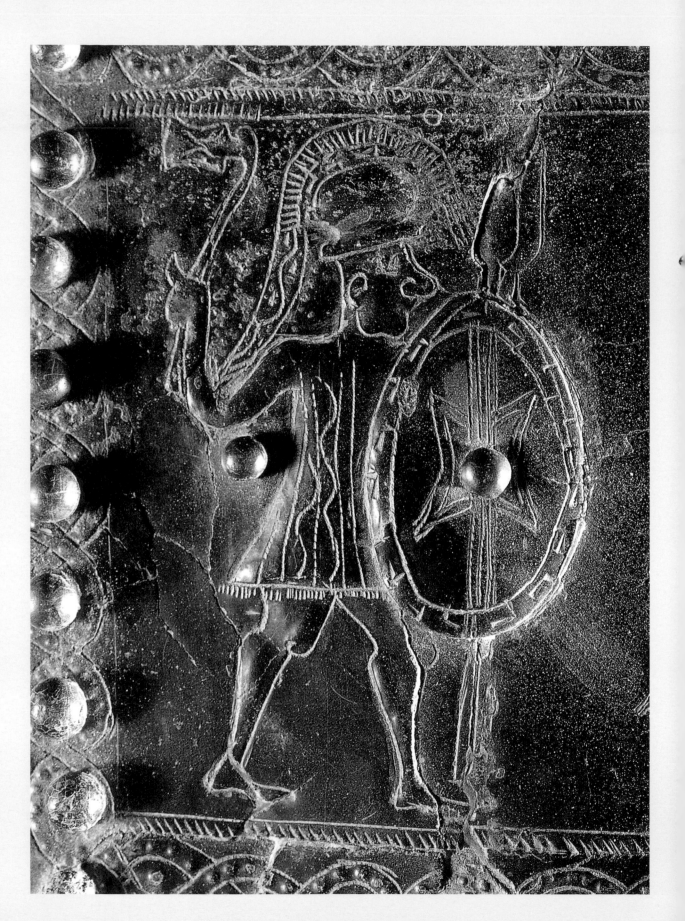

CHAPTER TWO

THE WARS
OF THE TRIBES
35,000–3200 BC

AN ILLYRIAN WARRIOR from the Balkans, c. 500 BC. For most of human history since the Upper Palaeolithic, warfare has been 'tribal', fought by groups below the level of the state and incapable of sustained policy. Nevertheless warfare has spurred a gradual increase in organizational complexity, culminating in the emergence in various places of full-time formal political leadership, usually in the form of a chief who can control lesser chiefs and nobles.

THE WARS OF THE TRIBES

THE ROLE OF WARFARE IN CULTURAL EVOLUTION

Charles Darwin, who picked his battlefields with care, avoided all mention of human evolution in *The Origin of Species* except for a brief reference at the end:

> In the distant future I see open fields for far more important researches. Psychology will be based on a new foundation, that of the necessary acquirement of each mental power and capacity by gradation. Light will be thrown on the origin of man and his history.

Twelve years later he entered those open fields himself in *The Descent of Man and Selection in Relation to Sex* (1871). In a chapter on the evolution of the intellectual and moral faculties he speculated at length on the functions of warfare:

> We can see, that in the rudest state of society, the individuals who were the most sagacious, who invented and used the best weapons and traps, and who were best able to defend themselves, would rear the greatest number of offspring. As a tribe increases and is victorious, it is often still further increased by the absorption of other tribes ... When two tribes of primeval man, living in the same country, came into competition, if (other circumstances being equal) the one tribe included a great number of courageous, sympathetic and faithful members, who were always ready to warn one another of danger, to aid and defend one another, this tribe would succeed better and conquer the other. Let it be borne in mind how all-important in the never-ceasing wars of savages, fidelity and courage must be.

Then Darwin asks how it is possible for 'a great number' of such courageous, sympathetic and faithful individuals to arise. Natural selection always promotes individual reproductive success, not the success of the group. Therefore altruistic traits like these, which induce individuals to sacrifice themselves for the group, ought to be eliminated by natural selection quite automatically. In the long run, of course, altruism will benefit the group, and hence the individuals who compose the group; but we need to explain how individuals with altruistic traits could be there in the first place. The evolution of altruistic behaviour has always been a central problem in Darwinian theory. It ought not to exist in a Darwinian world, yet it clearly does. And warfare, which tends to kill off the fittest young men before they have had much chance to reproduce, was one of the hardest altruistic behaviours to explain.

Darwin explained the evolution of altruism in three ways. Firstly, a human

Charles Darwin (1809–82). Early nineteenth-century evolutionary thought, under the influence of Jean-Baptiste Lamarck, assumed acquired characteristics were heritable. Darwin did not altogether abandon Lamarckism but he showed that the main mechanism of evolution is creative struggle, which he called natural selection.

society is capable of long memory and calculation, therefore it may deliberately select traits that benefit the group over the individual for utilitarian reasons: 'as the reasoning powers and foresight of the members became improved, each man would soon learn from experience that if he aided his fellow-men, he would commonly receive aid in return'. Secondly, utilitarian calculation might be supported by instinct, for habits 'followed during many generations probably tend to be inherited'. Finally, he suggested that natural selection had produced in ancestral humans an instinctive need for praise and aversion to blame from their fellows, though he could not explain exactly how.

However they started, these habits, once established in a tribe, would be propagated through natural selection, which at least in the human species can select for traits that benefit the group over the individual and hence can work on 'tribes' as if they were different species of animal:

It must not be forgotten that though a high standard of morality gives but a slight or no advantage to each individual man and his children over other men of the same tribe, yet that an increase in the number of well-endowed men and advancement in the standard of morality will certainly give an immense advantage to one tribe over another. There can be no doubt that a tribe including many members who, from possessing in a high degree the spirit of patriotism, fidelity, obedience, courage, and sympathy, were always ready to aid one another, and to sacrifice themselves for the common good, would be victorious over most other tribes; and this would be natural selection. At all times throughout the world tribes have supplanted other tribes; and as morality is one important element in their success, the standard of morality and the number of well-endowed men will thus everywhere tend to rise and increase.

This passage seems to be ignored by those who tell us Darwin was not a 'social Darwinist'.

To recapitulate an argument presented in the preceding chapter, recent neo-Darwinist thought has generally supported Darwin's speculations on the origins of warfare. The deepest cause of warfare is believed to be ethnocentricity, and this tendency probably arose in the way Darwin describes. Human evolution operates by a unique combination of the instinctive and the rational, and it has, to a large extent quite consciously, selected traits that benefit groups larger than the kin group. Darwin, like all scientists of his time, accepted the Lamarckian theory that acquired traits can be inherited, and therefore assumed the interaction between biology and culture could work both ways: instinct might promote habit, and habit in turn strengthen instinct. Modern biology has rejected Lamarckism, or the direct genetic inheritance of acquired cultural traits, but does accept the possibility of various tie-ins between cultural and genetic selection. If genetic tendencies to altruistic behaviour do exist, then a culture that encourages altruism should be a fertile ground for such genes, as Darwin suggested. Even without assistance from the genes, the process of cultural evolution by itself is capable of achieving fitness goals through deliberate cognitive manipulations and organized altruistic behaviours.

Moreover, Darwin thought warfare had been the main agent of cultural evolution. Nothing was then known about human origins except for the recently discovered bones of Neanderthal Man, and Darwin advanced no speculations about the matter; but he assumed that primitive man, from the time he split off from some apelike ancestor, was always an intelligent weapons-using species without natural predators, and therefore the main selection pressures in his evolution must have come from competition between one human group and another, which is to say from warfare. The science of anthropology did not yet exist, but Darwin did not need it to see that cultures resemble organisms or species, each with distinctive acquired traits that correspond to biological variations (or as we now say, mutations), that some of these are adaptive in that they promote the survival and reproduction of the culture, and that such cultural traits and the cultures that carry them will be preferred over others by the process of natural selection; and hence the evolution of the human moral and intellectual faculties, and every other sort of adaptive trait, especially those that lead to success in competition.

Probably most, even followers of the SSSM, would agree that warfare must have originally been a successful adaptation in the Darwinian sense. But the notion that warfare *continued* to be adaptive will meet with resistance. Darwin himself thought that under the conditions of modern civilization warfare was no longer a successful adaptation, but he thought it had been adaptive for a very long time. The concept of warfare as an instrument of group selection, of cultural evolution, and perhaps, in some ways, of progress was the core of social Darwinism. Modern social science has tried to avoid this disturbing thesis by every means possible, except refuting it. To evaluate it properly we must first review what is known about the history of warfare before the rise of civilized states.

FROM BAND TO TRIBE

Anthropologists distinguish four basic types of social organization, which they call the 'band', 'tribe', 'chiefdom', and 'state'. This division does not correspond exactly to the older classification into Old Stone Age hunting societies ('savages' as they were formerly called), New Stone Age agricultural societies (the former 'barbarians') and 'civilizations'. Some of the more complex hunting-and-gathering societies are considered to be 'tribes', and some complex Neolithic agricultural tribes are 'chiefdoms'.

'Bands' are the smallest and simplest of human societies: they usually number twenty to fifty people; they do not usually practise agriculture but live entirely by foraging over an immense and loosely defined territory; their social structure is extremely egalitarian. The examples known to Western ethnographers in recent centuries, such as the Eskimos, the Bushmen of southern Africa, the Congo Pygmies and the aborigines of the Australian interior, have inhabited grimly inhospitable environments and often seem to be relict or refugee populations. If they practise any warfare it is of very low intensity, for obvious reasons. In this category belong virtually all the known societies that can be described as genuinely peaceful, in that warfare and the cult

Australian aborigines lived in separate hunting-and-gathering bands, each an extended family or group of families, but neighbouring bands speaking related dialects would congregate once a year into a temporary macro-band of several hundred people to conduct ceremonies, trade, and marital arrangements.

of the warrior play no routine part in their culture and they avoid armed conflict with neighbours at all costs. These recent bands provide the closest analogue to the earliest human societies, but a dubious analogue because of their marginalized status. Unlike early Palaeolithic bands, these peoples live on the fringes of richer and more complex societies on which they are often dependent, and many of them are actually defeated and degraded 'tribes'.

Most of the primitive or pre-state peoples studied by anthropology are 'tribes'. A tribe is a group of bands or villages with a total membership usually in the hundreds. They live by foraging, agriculture, pastoralism, or some combination of these. In social structure they are practically as egalitarian as bands, but with more room for personal distinction, especially in warfare. They are united by pan-tribal associations such as warrior societies, or by a common language or related dialects, or by a myth of descent from a common ancestor. They co-operate, especially in war, and war chiefs may have much influence, but no one individual has power; decisions are made in council, usually by older males. This was probably the norm for human society between the Upper Palaeolithic cultural revolution and the growth of literate civilization, and when we speak of 'primitive warfare' we are almost always speaking of the tribal world, where it is a familiar institution.

About warfare in the Upper Palaeolithic there is very little to be said. There is ample evidence of homicide, but murder is not the same thing as war, and it is very difficult to find unmistakable archaeological evidence of warfare before the appearance of permanent settlements. The complexity of Upper Palaeolithic culture suggests the tribal stage of society. Band-level societies may have survived only in marginal areas, as they do today. We can infer the existence of tribal warfare, of the sort to be described shortly, but the vast dispersal of foraging peoples must have minimized competition and conflict. Space is the enemy of war. To slightly paraphrase Hobbes, it is in the nature of tribes to invade for safety, gain and glory; but not when they must travel days in order to do it, and there is little to gain in the absence of fixed settlements and stores, and, for the same reasons, little concern for safety; and as for glory, a culture must be fairly militarized to place a high value on it, which requires a certain level of military activity to begin with.

But the Upper Palaeolithic colonization of difficult environments such as the Arctic barrens, the tropical rainforests and the oceanic islands is a sign that the earth was filling up. After the end of the Ice Age, 12,000 years ago, there is evidence of more serious ecological change. Glaciers melted, seas rose, climates warmed, forests across northern Eurasia, the Middle East and north Africa began to dry up. The Upper Palaeolithic culture gave way to what archaeologists call the Mesolithic, in which there are signs of increasing population density and social complexity, with semi-permanent settlements in some places. From the Mesolithic comes the first definite evidence of warfare. In Offnet Cave in Germany a cache of thirty-four skulls of men, women and children was found,

brained with stone axes. This is significant because it proves that the practice of headhunting, which is later testified from all over the world, was already in vogue, and with it the cult of battle trophies as marks of prestige, and all that implies about the militarization of culture. At Jebel Sahaba in upper Egypt the skeletons of fifty-nine people killed with arrows were found, the possible record of a massacre. Cave paintings from Spain show the first pictorial representations of human combat, always with bow and arrow, and including a couple of group scenes, though whether of real or ritual battles is open to interpretation. The first real missile weapons, bow and sling and spear-thrower, became common at about this time; they would of course have been useful for hunting, but also extremely useful for warfare, as primitive warriors sensibly prefer missiles to shock weapons. Another invention was the axe or mace, a club with a stone head, which seems designed for the penetration of human skulls.

In south-west Asia the Mesolithic soon led to the Neolithic revolution. By 10,000 years ago there had appeared in the hills of Palestine, the southern

Mesolithic cave paintings from Spain, c. 10,000 BC, provide the earliest images of warfare. Most are hunting scenes, but two show human victims pierced by multiple arrows and two depict groups of archers in combat. This painting features some thirty warriors in a confused engagement.

Anatolian plateau and the Zagros range on the border between Iraq and Iran, a number of permanent mud-brick villages raising plots of barley, wheat and legumes and herding flocks of goats and sheep. By 8,000 years ago villages like these, some housing a few thousand people, dotted the Middle East and were spreading around the coasts of the Mediterranean.

Evidence for the prevalence of warfare in Neolithic societies is so well known that there seems no need to rehearse it in detail. In the regions most thoroughly

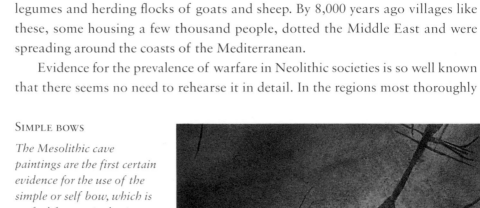

SIMPLE BOWS

The Mesolithic cave paintings are the first certain evidence for the use of the simple or self bow, which is crafted from a single piece of wood, usually a length of sapling. Several different types of simple bow are shown here, each in three positions – unstrung, strung, and drawn. These should be compared with the drawing of the composite bow on page 94. The simple bow has been called the first genuine machine made by man and its spread may have been the first evidence of the effects of serious warfare.

This rock painting from an Algerian cave shows a pitched battle between archers in the late Neolithic, 4000–1500 BC. The human figures are about 8 inches high. In tribal warfare pitched battles in the open are usually archery battles, shock weapons being reserved for more determined engagements.

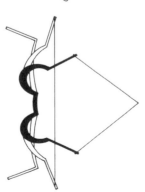

explored by archaeologists – the Middle East, Europe, North America – villages were commonly fortified with ditches, palisades, and walls, and often devastated by fire. Some burial sites are memorials of mayhem. At Talheim in Germany, 7,000 years ago, when farming was just beginning in northern Europe, some early farmers killed thirty-four people, half of them children, with stone axes and threw their bodies into a pit. The bloodiest Neolithic massacre site yet found is in the United States. At Crow Creek, South Dakota, a mass grave was unearthed

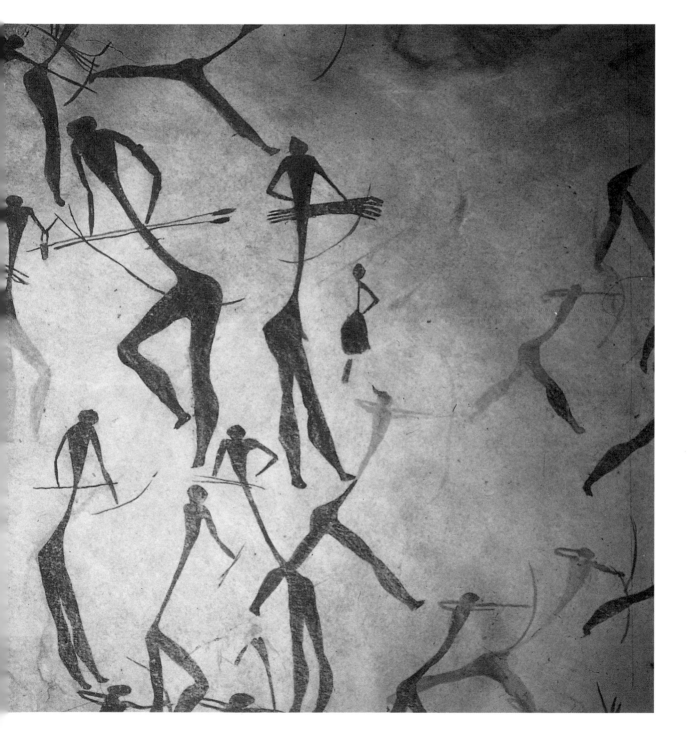

containing five hundred scalped and mutilated bodies, the inhabitants of a farming village on the Missouri River, which had been wiped from the earth one day around AD 1300.

The great Mesolithic/Neolithic transition – perhaps the most profound change in human history before the modern industrial revolution – is most plausibly explained as a result of human overpopulation. Often it is attributed to external ecological factors. We are told that the great beasts of the Ice Age became extinct at its close because of warming climate and overkill by human hunters, leaving no way to support the expensive Upper Palaeolithic lifestyle. But these changes were mostly confined to northern regions, and the Mesolithic/Neolithic transition was worldwide. On the cold steppes of Europe, the return of warmth and forest was unquestionably a disaster for the megafauna. Practically all the largest mammals died out – mammoth, elephant, rhinoceros, bison, giant elk, cave bear; the horse retreated to the eastern steppe and the reindeer to the northern steppe; the Mesolithic European hunter was left with the same selection of game animals that his medieval descendants pursued. But in the Middle East, which was mostly a temperate steppe in the Ice Age, there was little change in the fauna. The only megafauna were the Asian elephant and the hippopotamus, both of which survived far into historical times. The elephant herds of Syria would eventually succumb to overkill, but the hunters were Assyrian kings. And it was in the Middle East, not Europe, that the Neolithic was born.

Estimates of the human population of the earth at the close of the Palaeolithic range from 3 to 15 million. We do not know how Palaeolithic man judged the carrying capacity of his land, only that he needed a fantastic amount

The Yanomamo Indians, slash-and-burn agriculturalists, number only 10,000 souls scattered across a territory the size of Ohio, yet are almost constantly at war. The anthropologist Napoleon Chagnon, who has long studied them, concluded their wars are fought not for economic motives but for revenge, especially in quarrels over women.

of it by the standards of any humans now alive, and that by the late Palaeolithic he must have felt he was running out of it, because there is no other way to explain the discovery of America. It has been pointed out that foraging cultures can limit their populations, indeed have no choice about this because women kept on the move must space out their pregnancies or else accept the grim necessities of infanticide, at least through neglect. But this would not prevent a gradual, imperceptible rise in world population over many millions of years. The universal practice of exogamy would tend to equalize population. The ecological changes at the end of the Ice Age only accelerated a transition to a more crowded world that was already underway.

The general patterns of tribal warfare are well known and there is no reason to think they were different in the Stone Age. I will summarize here the principal features that distinguish tribal from state warfare, omitting for the moment societies at the chiefdom level, which may resemble states more than tribes. The most obvious difference is of course the small scale of tribal warfare. There are battles but no campaigns, tactics but no strategy, and the functions of leadership are mostly inspirational. There are ruses, such as the time-honoured feigned retreat and ambush, but only such as individual warriors can carry out; there are no massed formations capable of concerted manoeuvres. Pitched battles tend to have a ritualized or gamelike atmosphere, reminiscent of the cacophonous threat displays of baboon troops: the men meet by appointment at a designated battlefield and spend the day exchanging insults and missiles at extreme range, while the women form cheering sections in the rear and the old women scurry about shrieking curses at everybody, and the affair is broken off after a few casualties.

Tribal warfare should not, however, be seen as some kind of Homeric farce. These ritual battles are often only the initial stage of a war, and if they fail to settle the dispute, the war can easily escalate to much bloodier combats with hand-to-hand weapons. Formal battles, which affect only males, are the least destructive mode of tribal warfare. Tribesmen can also conduct murderous raids aimed at killing as many people as possible, regardless of age or sex. Though there are rarely many casualties from a single encounter, primitive wars can be more protracted than the wars of states, and we know of many cases where a tribe lost the majority of its warriors in the course of a war that may have dragged on for years. Among the warlike Yanomamo of Venezuela, one-third of the males meet their deaths in war. For a tribal people such casualty rates seem to be high but not extraordinary. Among civilized societies they are unknown, except for a few brief periods in the histories of some nations, such as Japan and Germany during the Second World War. The extinction of entire tribes is a fairly common event in the tribal world. New Guinea is an area of special importance here, because its traditional warfare continued into the 1950s, when the Australian government more or less stopped it, and has been the subject of much first-rate anthropological work. A recent study estimated that 10 per cent of the

OVERLEAF: *Warriors in full regalia from the Kawahari River region of New Guinea. In the New Guinea mountains wars often began with a ritual 'nothing fight' in which arrows were fired from a distance, but this could easily slide into a bloody 'true fight' with hand-to-hand weapons, or into ambush and massacre.*

57

ethnic groups in New Guinea have become extinct through warfare in *every* generation. (For the purposes of that study, 'ethnic group' was defined as any group that can conduct war.) Primitive war is small in scale but for that reason can be highly destructive.

As to the causes of war, there is a simple and significant difference. Primitive warfare, at least ostensibly, is about revenge. The reason tribal peoples commonly give for going to war is to avenge wrongs. The nature of the offence matters little. Women, assault, theft, sorcery, slander, and what we would call civil suits of every sort are all legitimate and common causes.

Some anthropologists have argued that the articulated aims of revenge and honour are only pretexts for materialistic motives, mainly territorial acquisition. In fact territorial changes are very frequent outcomes of tribal wars, and cases of tribal displacement, especially in desirable territories, may be found everywhere in anthropological literature. Surely no tribal war ever began without much hardheaded calculation of material costs and benefits. The best-known case of displacement may be the Nuer victory over the Dinka tribe in Sudan, because the former happened to become the subject of one of the classics of anthropological literature, E. E. Evans-Pritchard's *The Nuer* (1940). Over a seventy-year period the Nuer territory has expanded four times over, which is no mean territorial gain by any standard.

And yet one resists the conclusion that these wars were for 'economic' motives. Certainly all these peoples assumed that victory in a just war ought to bring some well-deserved material benefits to the victors, in addition to upholding their honour. But they were not accustomed to thinking in terms of abstractions like 'economic' and 'political' and had no authorities capable of the determination and sustained pursuit of such cold-blooded goals. A recent statistical study concluded that the most reliable predictor of warfare among tribal peoples is a history of unpredictable natural disasters; not real scarcity, as we might expect if the basic motives for war were economic, but, rather, a general sense of insecurity and vulnerability which intensifies fear of neighbours. If the fundamental cause of war is ethnocentric feeling, then it is the ultimate expression of the moral solidarity of the community, undertaken with the moral consensus of the people and their gods (who are often ancestors, hence the non-living portion of the community) to punish evil outsiders and defectors. War might serve many other functions as well, with no sense of contradiction; but a frankly predatory concept of warfare requires an extreme degree of pseudospeciation, of which tribal cultures rarely seem capable, and perhaps only when they encounter the utterly alien. The ethic of warfare set forth in Aristotle's *Politics* expresses an ancient and universal outlook: Aristotle assumed that wars between civilized peoples required the declaration of a just cause, and only against barbarians, fit to be slaves, could wars be waged for predatory reasons, as we would hunt wild animals. The horse nomads of the Eurasian steppe inspired utter terror precisely because they were capable of this attitude, regarding settled

A Dinka warrior of Sudan. The Dinka and Nuer are closely related pastoral tribes. The better-organized Nuer never had a deliberate strategy of expansion yet through persistent raiding have greatly expanded their grazing lands at the expense of the Dinka, in the process assimilating large numbers of Dinka captives.

peoples as beasts to be hunted; but they appeared late in history and in prehistoric times their equivalents may never have appeared at all. The worldwide custom of purification after battle, in which warriors perform expiatory rites to appease the ghosts of their slain enemies, is further testimony to the limits of pseudospeciation.

FROM CHIEFDOM TO STATE

During the several millennia that followed the spread of systematic agriculture the human population of the planet increased several times over. Demographic pressures eventually forced the growth of new layers of social complexity, including formal political authority. The earliest institutional political leadership doubtless took the form known to anthropology as a chiefdom. Chiefdoms are complex tribes with a ranked social structure, consisting of at least two ranks, the nobles and the commoners; and formal political leadership, usually in the form of a hereditary chief with religious and redistributive functions. These societies differ from states mainly in the absence of coercive bureaucracy, and this distinction can be a fine one.

The chiefs probably arose from among the 'big men' common in tribal cultures, who are mainly concerned with the redistribution of surplus wealth. The likely catalyst that turns 'big men' into chiefs is warfare. In peacetime the exploitative tendencies of an ambitious headman will be restrained by kinship and tribal custom, but prolonged warfare or the constant threat of it will give him opportunities to break free of these bonds and make his position absolute and hereditary. In the process the nature of war will change: permanent coercive leadership can channel group energies into sustained political and economic objectives; successful wars in turn bring new wealth and enlarge the redistributive functions of the chief. Chiefdoms may rule thousands or tens of thousands of people and may be more formidable in warfare than many states. Societies of this type have been common in recent centuries and they play a great part in anthropological literature, but that is because they typically flourish in the hinterlands of genuine states, which they imitate. The supreme examples of great chiefdoms were perhaps those of Polynesia in the eighteenth and nineteenth centuries, which were obviously indebted to European contacts. It is not easy to determine what chiefdoms were like in a world that had no states at all.

The chiefdom would appear to be a natural stepping stone to the state, except that normally it goes nowhere. The number of chiefdoms that evolved into states independently is miniscule: there are not above four examples in the Old World, and a couple of others in the New. This cannot be because they are ineffective in war. The historical chiefdoms have tended to be highly warlike and war-effective, sometimes capable of scoring victories over the mechanized armies of modern states. The last was in 1879, when the Zulus defeated the British at Isandlwana. Shaka (died 1828), the ruthless chief who founded Zulu power, was called by John Keegan 'a perfect Clausewitzian' because of the single-minded way he

The Zulus were originally a tribe of the Nguni people, cattle-raising pastoralists of southern Africa. In the early nineteenth century Shaka imposed a regimented military system: all males aged under 40 lived in barracks like the ancient Spartans, and were trained to fight in close formation with assegais (stabbing spears).

OVERLEAF: *A Zulu kraal (enclosed village). The Zulus originally practised the normal tribal warfare exemplified by the Nuer–Dinka conflict, but Shaka carried out a deliberate policy of conquest which spread chaos over a fifth of Africa. His military system was destroyed by the British in 1879. These photos were taken in the 1930s.*

Chiefdoms no longer exist. The best known examples were those of Polynesia and sub-Saharan Africa. Most of barbarian Europe contemporary with the ancient Middle Eastern civilizations was at the level of the chiefdom. This bronze sheet (fifth century BC) shows a warrior of the Venetic people of north-east Italy.

channelled all the energies of his primitive pastoral society into offensive warfare. Keegan suggests that the early demise of this power demonstrates the limitations of pure Clausewitzianism. Perhaps it was the limitation of chiefdoms in general to be too geared to the fluctuations of warfare and too unresponsive to the other needs of their societies. In Neolithic times they may have been uncommon and short lived. In the well-studied ethnographic history of the New Guinea highlands, an area densely populated by Neolithic standards where warfare and displacement have been common, there are many tribal 'big men', but none has ever become a chief, and if a chiefdom ever existed there it vanished without trace. The Zulu ascendancy was a response to overpopulation, exacerbated because their expansion to the south was blocked by the Dutch colonists in the Cape. Perhaps dynamic chiefdoms require such situations of entrapment.

There was, so to speak, something unnatural about the rise of political power. Unlike the development of agriculture and village life, which came independently in many different parts of the world, states arose in rare and special circumstances. During the first thousand years of recorded history this process took place only three times, in the basins of the Euphrates, Nile and Indus Rivers; and as the three rivers are not that far apart, the first provides the sole indisputable example in the Old World of a truly pristine civilization that owed nothing to external influences. Clearly there is that in human nature which resists centralized political power. It required a highly specialized environment for the process of political consolidation to continue to what, in retrospect, seems its predestined end.

These considerations have led to the widespread adoption of the 'circumscription' theory of state origins, which holds that advanced social complexity cannot evolve without population pressure in circumscribed agricultural land – a territory so enclosed by natural barriers that people cannot escape, creating a pressure-cooker effect. The three earliest examples fit that description, for all were alluvial river plains caged in by desert or dry steppe.

Neolithic population growth was dispersive: an expanding people acquired new land by replacing its neighbours and pushing them out into adjacent territories, as in the early-nineteenth-century Zulu expansion, an extreme case of tribal displacement whose effects were felt all over southern Africa. But in a completely caged environment, which in Neolithic times could only be created by geographical factors, population growth became aggregative and settlements mushroomed. In these human anthills the ancient social bonds stretched and snapped, to be replaced by a hierarchial organization, a central planning mechanism, in which the personal authority of the chief became stabilized, routinized and discretionary. There have been many attempts to identify the main cause or prime mover in this process. Two favourite suspects are irrigation and warfare: internal management and external defence. It seems likely the two worked together, indeed required one another, a process that will be examined more fully in the next chapter.

THE ARBITER OF HISTORY

But first let us return to the question of the role of warfare in human history. I will marshal what seem to me the most serious objections to the proposition that warfare has been a significant agent of cultural evolution.

First, history has no evolution in the Darwinian sense – that is to say, no functional adaptations that could not have come about by chance. As the anthropologist C. R. Hallpike puts it:

> in small-scale societies with simple technologies there are many ways of organizing social relations and of adapting to the environment, and within very broad limits they will all work. This being so, it is futile to try to explain any of them as some kind of optimal strategy for anything, and the reason they exist will be a matter of historical contingencies.

An Aztec god slays an ocelot warrior (Codex Cospi, fifteenth century AD). The Aztec empire was the most militaristic of pre-Columbian states, but there was a curious ceremonial quality to its warfare. Battles were fought mostly to take captives for human sacrifice, and cities were unfortified.

Many social scientists and probably most historians would subscribe to this view. There are, however, reasons to think that there have been very long-range evolutionary trends in history, so long-range that most historians, who work within very limited time spans, never notice them. Since the Upper Palaeolithic, human society has not only grown steadily in social complexity, but has everywhere grown in the same directions. In the Old World these parallel trends might be attributed to diffusion, but in the New World, where there was no possibility of significant contact between 40,000 BC and AD 1492, society developed along the same path, from band to tribe to chiefdom to state; and the history of warfare in the New World followed the same course as in the Old, the main differences being clearly attributable to the absence of any beasts suitable for riding or pulling chariots. The anthropologist Marvin Harris pointed out that 'the story of the second earth shows that cultural evolution has not resulted

Mayan vase with battle scenes. The vanquished are distinguished by their flower ornaments. The wars of Mesoamerican civilizations, compared to their ancient Eurasian counterparts, preserved a primitive ritual character, which may be related to the absence of horses. Offensive war in the Old World required chariots and cavalry.

in a chaotic jungle of contradictory and unique events, but in … massive parallel and converging trends'.

It is true that most of the cultural variations spread by warfare are not particularly adaptive in the Darwinian sense. If a victorious tribe should absorb all its rivals, they are all likely to adopt its taboo against, say, the eating of shellfish, although this custom is in no way contributory to the tribe's success, is not particularly beneficial for survival and reproduction, and indeed may be maladaptive. The vast majority of cultural traits, such as preferences for one hairstyle or pottery design over another, are not functional adaptations for competition with other groups, and many seem obviously maladaptive, such as the disfiguring and dangerous ritual mutilations common in the tribal world. They succeed because they are 'functional' in the sense that anthropologists usually interpret the word: adaptive in terms of their own cultural milieu, though not necessarily making sense anywhere else. But this is equally true of biological evolution. The great majority of genetic variations are not especially adaptive, and often non-adaptive traits are propagated by accident, because they happen

to be associated with adaptive traits, a phenomenon called 'hitchhiking' by geneticists. According to evolutionary theory the adaptive traits should still win out over the long run. There is no obvious reason why cultural evolution should not produce the same result. *Some* cultural variations should be sufficiently adaptive to ensure that their carriers are consistently 'victorious over most other tribes', regardless of historical contingencies; and this, as Darwin said, 'would be natural selection'.

Second, if there have been parallel and convergent trends, these have not been caused by group extinctions. It is true that group extinction could not be the only cause. It was argued above that the worldwide shift from hunting to farming, which has been called the most conspicuous testimonial to the power of Darwinian cultural adaptation, was a reaction to a worldwide demographic swell. Agriculture can support a population density fifty times that of a foraging economy, so foragers must eventually be pushed out or be absorbed by farmers. But foragers are not helpless to retard this process, especially in its initial stages. Even in the age of railroad and rifle, the Great Plains of North America could not

Navajos in the Arizona Territory, 1880s. As late as the time of the Anglo-Zulu War the Indian tribes of the western prairies and deserts, who possessed no chiefdom remotely as formidable as the Zulu, were still capable of keeping white settlers off their lands, and it required the armies of a major industrial power to remove them.

be put to agricultural uses until their indigenous foragers had been removed by military means. Much the same can be said about other massive trends, such as the rise of the state. In speaking of cultural evolution, 'extinction' normally means the sociocultural, not the physical, termination of a group; but it is still difficult to see how any kind of evolution can proceed unless some groups disappear and others survive and replicate themselves.

Warfare is not the only cause of group extinction. The red horseman rarely rides alone. But warfare is the decisive cause and often administers the final blow to a group already weakened by malnutrition, disease, or desertion. It is not clear from the anthropological data that any culture, except perhaps insular populations small enough to be wiped out by one hurricane, has ever become totally extinct without the assistance of human enemies. The disappearance of the Norse colony in Greenland in the late Middle Ages, an extinction both cultural and physical, has been attributed to worsening climate in an environment already marginal; but there is archaeological evidence that the settlement finally succumbed to Eskimo raids.

The modern European invasion of America has been a success. The medieval invasion failed utterly, leaving a bleak monument in the ruins of the Norse eastern settlement in Greenland, founded c. AD 1000 and abandoned in the fifteenth century. The legends of the Greenland Eskimo recall that their ancestors wiped out the invaders.

Third, rates of group extinction are too slow to account for significant cultural change. It may be recalled that Darwin thought that the 'never-ceasing wars of savages' was a necessary backdrop to cultural evolution. The New Guinea data referred to above, however, indicates an average rate of group extinction so slow that the compilers of that study estimated it would take between 500 and 1,000 years for serious cultural changes to take place.

The real rates of change, however, must be far faster than that. The most important difference between cultural and biological evolution is that cultural groups can select favourable adaptations deliberately, without waiting for the lumbering processes of group extinction. Though the innate conservatism of ethnocentricity inhibits cultural borrowing, people can sometimes foresee the eventual results of group selection and act to forestall them. When the first tribe took up archery, its rivals probably, and in short order, did the same thing, realizing that otherwise they would be pushed into marginalization or extinction. The threat of war may be a more potent agent of cultural change than its practice. Clausewitz said battle need not be offered often, and in fact the prudent commander will enter into it rarely, but it is still to military activity what cash payment is in business affairs. Likewise, the advantage of warfare over all other modes of group competition is that of cash over credit.

The fourth and last point is that Machiavellian intelligence is self-defeating. There is about it something almost deliberately anti-evolutionary. Cultures, unlike genes, are calculating and devious entities that are normally fated to contend with rivals as cunning as themselves. The strategies of cultural evolution cannot depend upon accumulated experience and are not played with a passive environment. The strategies must be as fluid as in a chess game; the environment that counts is social, intelligent, reactive; the only thing that can be predicted is that any improvement in skill will select for a corresponding improvement in the other players. It is the most challenging of games and it can produce brilliant moves, but it leads very easily to stalemate. Hence the rules of Machiavelli constantly defeat those of Darwin, and the normal outcome of war is a balance of power, which is the opposite of evolution.

For the reasons given above, and especially the last, warfare must normally have been a somewhat inefficient agent of cultural evolution. It cannot have accounted for most cultural change, nor could it have provided much of a check on the limitless proliferation of cultural variations, which otherwise would not be as diverse as they undoubtedly are. Nevertheless it is difficult to resist the conclusion that in the final analysis warfare has been a decisive arbiter in human evolution, both biological and cultural; and it has been so not only in the great crises of prehistory, but also in many important breakthroughs within historical times. Several such breakthroughs will be examined in the chapters that follow.

Niccolò Machiavelli (1469–1527), Florentine diplomat and historian, formulated the theory of raison d'état *that goes by his name. Machiavellian intelligence is the ability to design scenarios to ensure evolutionary success. The 'strategies' of natural selection are unconscious; those of cultural selection are deliberate.*

CHAPTER THREE

THE WARS OF THE CITIES 3200–1700 BC

*A detail from the Stele of the Vultures, c. 2450 BC
(see p. 82). In the top register the men of Lagash, protected
by huge overlapping shields and helmets of metal or leather,
advance over the bodies of their Ummaite enemies. The
number of heads, hands, and feet do not match because the
sculptor has attempted to portray a body of soldiers in deep
formation. Probably each shield had a single boss; the shields
are depicted with six bosses each to suggest the men are
drawn up in six ranks. On the bottom register, Eanatum,
king of Lagash, charges in his 'chariot'.*

THE WARS OF THE CITIES

SUMERIAN WARFARE

The oak-covered hills to the east and north of the Tigris–Euphrates valley were home to some of the earliest agricultural sites, but farmers long avoided the baked plains except to hunt onager and gazelle. Not until 5000 BC did villages and irrigation channels appear along the two great rivers. Archaeologists call this the Ubaid culture, after one of its early sites. Nothing dramatically new developed until 3500 BC, when there grew up in the very fertile down-river plain, later known as Sumer, an offshoot of the Ubaid known as the Uruk culture, after another archaeological site. Soon this became the first culture that can be

The oldest massive fortifications in the world are those of Jericho near the Dead Sea. Stone walls 12 feet high and 6 feet thick, with high towers, were erected c. 7500 BC around an oasis that was home to 2,000 inhabitants. Later in the Neolithic fortifications became common around the Middle East.

described as urban, with a probable majority of its people living in walled towns with populations in the thousands. Sometime late in the fourth millennium a point of take-off was reached in cultural complexity. We may imagine growing up along the riverbanks a series of core areas of productive irrigated land, each united by patron–client relationships to a periphery of farming villages and pastoralists, each forming a network of economic redistribution controlled by a managerial élite in the central town. The whole network resembled a great household, and from an early time was conceived simply as the household of the god who resided in the main temple, while the human governors were thought of as the god's stewards. Towards 3000 BC the Uruk culture entered a climactic phase that can be described as the first civilization: populations became densely concentrated in the central towns; wheeled vehicles and bronze weapons were

The first writing, undecipherable to us, appeared in the late Uruk period (3500–3000 BC). By c. 3000 BC this had developed into a cuneiform (wedge-shaped) script, inscribed with a reed on clay tablets, which can be read as Sumerian. Used mostly for accounts, it is one of the signs that complex urban organization had emerged.

fashioned; temples – awesome by any previous standard – were erected; chiefs were buried in tombs that deserve the adjective 'royal'; and the first messages were written on clay tablets. Warfare must have played an important part in this process. As the Sumerian Plain, which is the size of Belgium or New Jersey, filled up with the complex communities described above, disputes of the usual Neolithic sort would have proliferated, more frequent and more serious now because they were increasingly focused on rights over land and water, and these rivalries must have contributed to the consolidation of the new élites in the towns. It is plausible to imagine an early period of fairly intensive warfare in Sumer, resembling in scale the warfare of the more advanced chiefdoms, which culminated in the consolidation of the city states early in the third millennium.

During the Early Dynastic Age (2900–2350 BC) Sumer contained some thirty such cities. At any given time there were a dozen or more major cities, each with its imposing temple and patron deity, each controlling an agricultural territory stretching for some miles around its walls. Some

EARLY MESOPOTAMIA AND SYRIA 4300–2300 BC

It is widely thought that the ancient coastline of the Gulf extended much further north than now; hence this map puts Ur on the coast. After the rise of the Akkadian Empire c. 2300 BC southern Mesopotamia was called 'Sumer and Akkad'. 'Akkad' probably referred to the largely Semitic northern area. The civilization of Elam, which achieved literacy almost as early as Sumer, was cut off from it by the marshes of the Gulf. Sumerians called northern Mesopotamia 'Subartu'.

cities were within sight of another's walls. The largest cities had populations of perhaps 50,000; the population of all Sumer is reckoned at half a million.

The primary source for unravelling the early history of these cities is the *Sumerian King List*, a document compiled around 2000 BC which purports to list all the kings who had held the position of *nam-lugal*, high king, over Sumer. According to this text the gods first set up kingship at Eridu (known from archaeology to have been an ancient centre of the Ubaid culture), where two kings reigned for 64,800 years between them. The supreme kingship was then held in succession by four other cities, and by kings of comparable longevity, for the next 176,000 years. Then the gods sent a great Flood which drowned all men but one. After the Flood a new start was made, and once again kingship was 'lowered from heaven', this time at Kish, where twenty-three kings reigned 24,510 years, three months and three and a half days. Here we touch dry land, for Kish was a place of mysterious importance in later times, and the title 'King of Kish' always conveyed a claim to hegemony in Mesopotamia. The last two kings of the First Dynasty of Kish in the *King List* are historical figures, the first attested by an inscription and the second by literature: 'En-mebaragesi, the one who carried

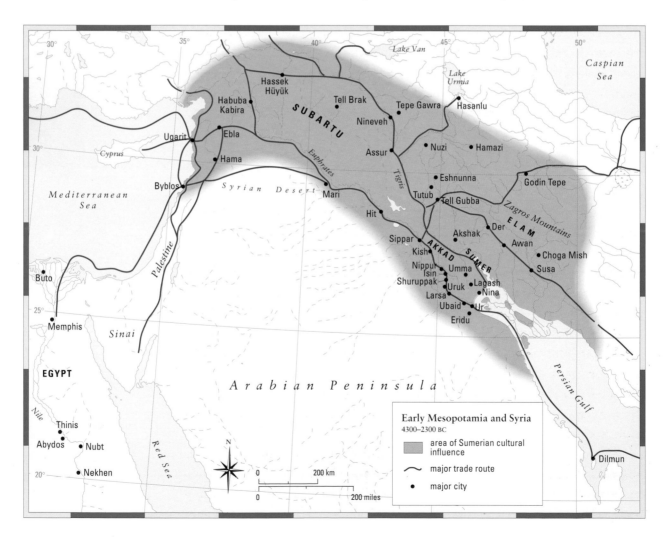

Early Mesopotamia and Syria
4300–2300 BC

▨ area of Sumerian cultural influence

∿ major trade route

• major city

away as spoil the weapons of the land of Elam [south-west Iran], became king and reigned 900 years; Akka, son of En-mebaragesi, reigned 625 years.' After Akka, 'Kish was smitten with weapons' and its kingship passed to Uruk, one of whose early kings was named Gilgamesh. In the epic poem *Gilgamesh and Akka*, Akka of Kish appears as the enemy of Gilgamesh, whose city Uruk is unsuccessfully besieged by Akka. Gilgamesh of Uruk, who became the Sumerian folk hero and the subject of many epic tales, was doubtless an historical person who lived in the twenty-seventh century. After Uruk the kingship passed to Ur, a city well known from its inscriptions. From this time on, the *King List* becomes more historical and the life spans of its rulers more credible, and it can be supplemented not only by inscriptions on stone but by archival and literary texts on clay.

As the *King List* shows, the Sumerians assumed that 'The Land', as they called it, was of almost inconceivable antiquity and had always been ruled by many city kings under a single high king. The notion which gave the *King List* its organizing principle, that only one city at a time had held the supreme kingship, with no overlap, is obviously fictive; but when this was written exact chronology was a novel idea and the compilers may have known no other way to organize their material. The *King List* is also selective: Lagash, because of its extensive inscriptions, is the best known to us of all Sumerian cities, and we know that in the twenty-fifth century its king styled himself 'King of Kish' and held a sort of hegemonic position in Sumer; yet Lagash never appears in the List and we can only guess at the reasons for the omission. But the myth of unity was supported by the common pantheon and by the centrality of the temple city of Nippur, which was never a city state and had no kings, yet no one was recognized as *nam-lugal* unless he had been confirmed by Enlil, king of the gods, at Nippur.

The Sumerians believed that there had always been kings, and there is no sound reason to doubt it. Some modern authorities have supposed the cities were originally ruled by priesthoods and have seen in the titles *ensi* and *lugal*, the usual terms for rulers, a distinction between priestly and royal functions; but Sumerian kingship was so theocratic that the distinction seems unclear, and the different titles may have reflected only regional differences. Others have thought, on the basis of occasional references to assemblies and councils, that the cities originally had a republican form of government and that monarchy arose later; but it is more plausible to see in these advisory bodies a vestige of the primitive tribal consensus, and to imagine city kingship growing directly out of the Neolithic chiefdom with no republican detour. Republican government, it will be argued later, assumes a type of social structure that did not appear until the first millennium BC.

Warfare was clearly an important feature of the Early Dynastic world. The *King List* assumes that the title of *nam-lugal* usually passed from one city to another by warfare. Sooner or later the leading city was 'smitten with weapons' and its hegemony passed to another. All the chief Sumerian gods had military

Terracotta relief, c. 2000 BC, featuring the goddess of sex and of war, Inanna, called Ishtar by Semites, wearing a crown of lunar horns and a rainbow necklace, accompanied by her lions and owls. At the New Year ceremony the king of the city played the role of her lover Dumuzi (Tammuz) and somehow had sexual union with her.

functions: Enlil, the high god, was 'he who breaks the enemy like a reed'; the goddess of love, Inanna, was also goddess of war. The functions of the king, who was simply the deputy of the chief god of the city, were largely concerned with warfare. Fighting warriors and bound captives appear frequently in Sumerian art. But it is very difficult to determine what early Sumerian wars – the first wars between states in human history – were like, and the common assumption that they resembled the state-level warfare of later times may be misleading.

Though Sumer emerged into a sort of historical half-light by around 2600 BC, the only city rivalry about which we have much information is that between Lagash and Umma, cities located 18 miles apart, which were repeatedly in conflict over a disputed piece of irrigated land on their borders. Lagash recorded its claims on a series of inscriptions. These tell us that about 2600 BC the dispute had been arbitrated and the boundary demarcated by the current *nam-lugal*, Mesalim, king of Kish. But sometime after 2500 BC Ush, king of Umma, invaded the disputed territory and smashed the boundary stone Mesalim had put up. Then Ningirsu, the chief god of Lagash, appeared in a dream to Eanatum, king of Lagash, and ordered him to restore the god's 'beloved field', promising him that Umma would be abandoned by its ally Kish and that the king of Umma would be killed by his own people. (All wars were fought to avenge the honour of

Stone wall plaque bearing a portrait of Enanatum, king of Lagash c. 2400 BC. He was the brother of Eanatum, the king who put up the Stele of the Vultures, and probably met defeat at the hands of the king of Umma. Plaques of this sort may have been votive objects. See also the votive plaque of his grandfather Ur-Nanshe on p. 108.

the god, as simpler societies fight to avenge the honour of the people; a king went to war at the command of his god, who naturally possessed good intelligence about shifts in the balance of power and the internal affairs of enemy cities.) In both of the two battles that followed, Lagash was victorious over Umma, or rather, as the inscriptions present the matter, Ningirsu defeated Shara the god of Umma. Ningirsu 'cast the great battle-net' of Enlil over the Ummaites and erected twenty burial mounds over fallen Ummaites in the plain. Ush seems to have been overthrown by his own people as prophesied, and a treaty was made with his successor in which the Ummaite king promised to pay tribute and neither trespass on Ningirsu's land nor alter the irrigation channels. The treaty was sealed by a ritual of obscure significance in which six pairs of doves, their heads crowned with cedar and their eyes marked with kohl, were released to six temples in six different cities. A later king of Umma, Urluma, acquired new allies and repossessed the disputed land; the then king of Lagash, Enanatum (Eanatum's brother), fought with him and, since the inscriptions do not mention the result, was probably defeated. But Enanatum's son Enmetena defeated Urluma, captured sixty of his ass teams and put up five burial mounds over his fallen soldiers, while Urluma was killed in Umma by his own people.

The inscriptions tell us much about the treaties but nothing about the fighting itself, except that Eanatum was wounded by an arrow. The theocratic conventions of Middle Eastern royal inscriptions always precluded anything resembling realistic battle description. There are no real battles, only routs and massacres. But Eanatum also commemorated his victory in bas-relief on the Stele of the

The Stele of the Vultures, so called from the birds eating the bodies of the dead, was originally put up in a temple by Eanatum. It was found in fragments, which are now in the Louvre. On the top register Eanatum marches ahead of his men on foot. On the bottom register he leads them standing in an ass-drawn cart.

Vultures, which is one of the two main pictorial sources for Early Bronze Age warfare. The other is the so-called Standard of Ur, a plaque of unknown purpose made about 2500 BC and found in the Royal Tombs of Ur. On the basis of these two works, it has been supposed that Sumerian armies included war chariots and phalanxes of heavy infantry. This is to read back into the dawn of interstate warfare two institutions that appeared very much later.

The war chariot was an invention of the High Bronze Age, after 1700 BC. The disciplined formation of heavy infantry was invented by the Archaic Greeks, and Eastern armies first met it in the fifth century BC. Both chariotry and phalanx, when they finally appeared, were devastating innovations that revolutionized

SUMERIAN BATTLE CART

Artist's reconstruction of the Sumerian battle cart. The wheels were solid wood and there was no swivelling front axle, making it impossible for the vehicle to turn quickly. The asses were controlled by rings in their upper lips, which does not suggest high training. Yet there is evidence for palace departments specializing in the care of these animals.

Excavations at Ur in 1927–32 uncovered the Early Dynastic Royal Tombs, the most spectacular find in Mesopotamian archeology. The treasures, now in the British Museum, included this ceremonial gold helmet, which resembles the helmet worn by Eanatum on the Stele of the Vultures.

warfare, which makes it unlikely they had been around since the beginning of civilization. The 'war chariot', which is pictured both on the Stele and the Standard, is a most improbable vehicle, a heavy wagon pulled by what look like onagers (the Asian wild ass, *Equus hemionus*); but as this beast has always been found totally untamable, they are perhaps onagers crossed with domestic donkeys (*E. asinus*). Whatever they are, they are guided by rings in their noses, and the king they are pulling is armed with throwing spears, not a bow such as the real charioteers of the High Bronze Age invariably carried. It is impossible to imagine this contraption being used in battle. It was clearly a prestige vehicle. The fact that the Ummaites left sixty of them on the battlefield demonstrates that any man of rank had to have one, and that they were of little use when it came to making an escape.

The foot soldiers are a much more serious proposition, but to compare them with the Greek hoplites of 2,000 years later is to be struck by the lightness of their equipment: wooden shields, light metal helmets, no metal body armour, though sometimes a corselet of leather or canvas seems to be worn. On the Stele they are drawn up several ranks deep, which does make them resemble a phalanx. On the other hand, given a horde of hundreds of men to organize, there is nothing much one can do with them except form them into ranks, so that they would inevitably look something like a phalanx. It is not obvious from these representations what they were supposed to do on a battlefield.

It will be more enlightening to look at siege warfare, the only kind of Early Bronze Age warfare for which we have substantial archaeological evidence. Practically all the large city mounds that have been excavated in Mesopotamia

The 'Standard' of Ur is a wooden object inlaid with elaborate scenes in shell and lapis lazuli. The battle scenes show soldiers with heavy cloaks instead of shields, and ass carts charging over the bodies of the enemy dead, which was probably all they ever did in battle. The other side shows banquet scenes.

ARROWHEADS

A flint arrowhead from Egypt (top right). Stone weapons continued in use in Old Kingdom Egypt, a testimony to its military backwardness. Bronze arrowheads from Assyria (bottom) and Iran (top left). By the later Bronze Age arrowheads were forged with a central spine to pierce armour.

Ancient missile weapons fired more rapidly than any firearms available before the late nineteenth century AD but had lower impact, so shields could provide sufficient protection. Slings were probably more lethal than simple bows but only in the hands of specialists. These bronze arrowheads were found on the battlefield of Carchemish (605 BC).

reveal the foundations of elaborate fortifications erected around the beginning of the Early Dynastic period. These urban fortifications are strong evidence for the consolidation of centralized political authority at this time. At about the same time the techniques of civilization were spreading to north Mesopotamia, Syria and Palestine, and there too fortifications everywhere testify to the formation of city states. By 2500 BC, one of these cities, Ebla in northern Syria, was writing its Semitic language in a script derived from Sumerian cuneiform, and has left archives suggesting a kingdom of considerable size. The walls of Mesopotamian cities were of mud-brick; those of the Levant might be of stone, or at least have stone foundations. All the foundations are enormously thick; those of Ur measure 100 feet at the base. This is because earthen walls must have a base the thickness of which is at least one-third the height of the tapering wall. Babylonian texts from the second millennium BC indicate that it was common for Mesopotamian cities to be surrounded by walls 60 feet high. Often walls were built in a zigzag pattern, often studded with towers or bastions spaced every 100 feet or so, so that archers and slingers in the towers could cover the entire wall with flanking fire.

These defences are of course conclusive proof that cities lived in fear of siege, and the height of the walls suggests that in the beginning the usual method of storming a city was by escalade. A scaling ladder could not be more than 30 feet

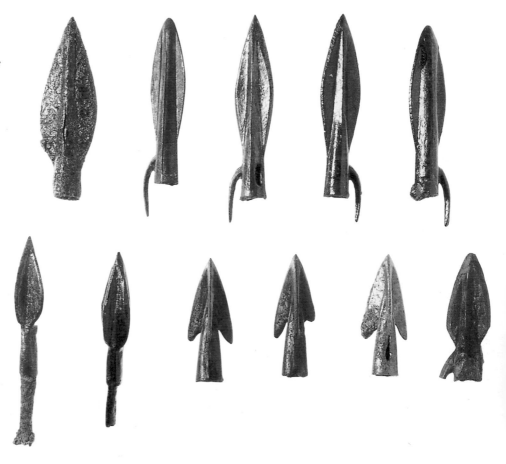

long or it could not easily be transported, so a wall more than 30 feet high should be reasonably secure from escalade. In that event it would be necessary to breach the wall. The earliest representation of siege warfare is a sculpture from Deshashe in Egypt, from the twenty-seventh century, which shows soldiers storming a walled city, probably in Palestine, by a combination of scaling and breaching: some are climbing walls under covering fire from archers, while others are prising at the wall with long poles. An Egyptian painting from Kaemheset (twenty-third century) shows a siege in which scaling ladders are equipped with wheels to make it easier to position the ladder, and men standing on a ladder are pounding on the wall with axes. Against walls of adobe brick, poles and axes might be fairly effective tools, but the use of such implements means that the battering ram had not yet been invented, and the prospect of working through an immense wall by these methods under a rain of arrows and stones from the battlements does not seem inviting. Moreover, city walls were sometimes constructed in unbonded sections so that if one section collapsed it would not pull down the whole wall.

The contrast between the relatively advanced state of fortification and the relatively primitive state of armies, which represented hardly any advance over the Neolithic except for the use of metals, induces one to suggest that Early Dynastic warfare was basically siege warfare. If an invading army were superior in

The damaged limestone relief at Deshashe. On the left, Egyptians with axes and bows fight long-haired Canaanites and on the bottom register, take them prisoner. On the right, Egyptians storm a Canaanite city. Its walls, viewed from above, have semicircular bastions. Beneath the scaling ladder men prise at the gate with poles.

numbers, a king might not offer battle at all but stay behind his walls, as Gilgamesh did when the land of Uruk was invaded by Akka of Kish. In the *Gilgamesh and Akka* epic, which was written in post-Sargonic times but may contain authentic traditions about Early Dynastic warfare, Akka makes no attempt to storm the walls of Uruk. The warriors of Uruk gather at the gate and appear to be preparing to charge out and offer battle to the besiegers, but instead the leaders parley and a treaty is arranged. The invader might try to devastate crops, but this is so difficult to do under the conditions of ancient agriculture that the threat would be mostly symbolic unless the invader could manage to invade precisely at harvest time. If battle were offered, one doubts that it involved any proper *formations* of infantry at all. Instead of charges en masse, with shields locked together in the fashion developed much later by the Greeks, we should imagine an individualistic Neolithic mêlée with plenty of room for the men to keep out of one another's way, for that is what fighting with hand-to-hand weapons tends to amount to in the absence of tight disciplined formations. The powerful composite bow was not yet in use, so arrows and slings were not very effective against men protected by big shields, metal helmets and studded cloaks. In Sumerian art bows normally appear in hunting scenes, rarely in warfare. The best representation of archery in war is a carving from Mari showing an archer protected by a spearman with a large wicker shield, clearly during a siege. Battles were probably uncommon, and when they occurred, short in duration and light in casualties, since the defenders always had the option of retreating behind the city walls. The twenty burial mounds Eanatum erected after his great victory suggest a few hundred Ummaites were killed in battle or executed afterwards; but this battle may have been exceptional, as its unique commemoration on stone suggests. His nephew Enmetena claimed only five mounds, and an earlier Lagashite king about 2500 BC claimed victories over Umma and Ur with only one mound each.

The pursuers might hope to get inside the walls before the gates were closed, but usually a siege would be necessary. The real use of missiles was to attack and protect the besiegers; the function of the spearmen was to force a way through a gate or breach in the wall, which may be what Eanatum's ranked infantry on the Stele of the Vultures are trying to do. It is doubtful that any Sumerian city state possessed the manpower to conduct a long siege, without which no city properly supplied could be starved into submission; and given the absence of effective rams or other storming techniques, the defenders of a well-fortified city would seem to have possessed a clear advantage over the besiegers. One may suppose that the fall of a city was accompanied by sack because that is a universal practice, but one suspects that before Sargon of Akkad the sack of a city was an extremely rare event. In the Lagash–Umma wars the defeated city appears to surrender on terms, and this was probably a typical outcome. Surrender might be facilitated by the deposition of the defeated king. Treaties sometimes ended with a formulaic curse calling for the king who breaks his oath to be overthrown and killed by his own people in his own city.

There is not much information about the way armies were organized. Kings doubtless had their hand picked guards, but large armies must have been conscript armies. Much of the land was owned by temples, which contributed men from their tenantry for military and other services. We hear of a big temple at Lagash that furnished five hundred soldiers to the king. An inscription from Shuruppak mentions six hundred soldiers going into battle. Armies seem to have numbered in the hundreds or at most a few thousand. Alliances between cities were clearly of fundamental importance, as it probably required a formidable coalition to carry out a successful siege. Hence we can dimly discern the familiar pattern of a constantly shifting balance of power accompanied by much intrigue and occasional warfare. There was nothing new about any of this; Neolithic tribes behaved likewise.

It is impossible to say how common inter-city warfare in Sumer may have been, as the stone monuments that reveal the Lagash–Umma conflict have rarely survived; but one is left with a strong impression that the warfare of the earliest civilization, however frequent, was rarely a very serious or decisive affair, not at least if it concerned strongly fortified cities with approximately equal manpower resources. In a typical war of this sort we should perhaps imagine a short and inconclusive engagement in the open, followed by a longer but equally inconclusive siege operation, and then a treaty. If the stakes of war amounted to nothing but a disputed stretch of irrigated field, the victor would then be free to occupy it. If the stakes included the title of *nam-lugal*, which was expected to pass from one city to another by war, a symbolic victory may have sufficed, since the *nam-lugal* seems to have held a mostly symbolic position, with nothing much to do but arbitrate disputes upon request. The ideology reflected in the *Sumerian King List* views Sumer as a closed and balanced political system, permanently divided into divinely sanctioned city states with divinely sanctioned boundaries; intermittent struggle among them is taken for granted, but neither conquest nor unification is envisioned. This city-state ideology probably corresponded to political reality.

Not all wars involved neighbouring cities. Eanatum of Lagash declared in his inscriptions that he conducted raids as far away as Elam, perhaps for tribute, perhaps to bolster his claim to the title king of Kish. And the irrigated land had to be defended from pastoralists, but since nomads without horses or camels could have been no great threat this may be envisioned as a police activity.

The hypothesis put forward here is that Sumerian city states at an early date in the third millennium became capable of carrying out wars for sustained economic and political objectives, but these objectives were almost immediately frustrated by the sudden development of the art of fortification. The stalemated cities then settled down to a type of warfare that probably represented a regression from the Neolithic, as it seems to have been less serious and destructive than the typical warfare of advanced chiefdoms. This pattern then endured for some centuries.

THE AKKADIAN EMPIRE

The pattern was broken some time after 2400 BC, when some kings began to dream of gains more lucrative than a neighbouring irrigation ditch, and glories more refulgent than the empty title of *nam-lugal*. The first would-be-imperialist was Lugalzagesi, king of Umma. First he settled scores with the old enemy Lagash, taking the city, burning its temples and carrying away treasures in gold and lapis lazuli. A clay tablet survives in which a scribe of Lagash calls on the gods, both of Lagash and Umma, to avenge this sacrilege, which may have been a thing unheard of in Sumer. Lugalzagesi then became king of Ur and of Uruk; the latter city became his base, for he appears in the *King List* as constituting, all by himself, the Third Dynasty of Uruk. He is said to have had fifty *ensi* (rulers or governors) under him. When he won recognition from Nippur as *nam-lugal*, he dedicated vases in the temple of Enlil bearing the following inscription:

> When to Lugal-zagesi – King of Uruk, King of the Land [a long list of titles follows].... Enlil, king of countries, had given the Kingship of the Land, made the Land obedient to him, thrown all countries at his feet, and subjected them to him from sunrise to sunset – at that time he made his way from the Lower Sea [the Persian Gulf], via the Tigris and Euphrates, to the Upper Sea [the Mediterranean], and Enlil had allowed none to oppose him from sunrise to sunset. Under him all countries lay contented in their meadows, and the Land rejoiced. The shrines of Sumer, the Governors of all countries and the region of Uruk decreed the role of ruler for him. At that time Uruk spent the days in celebrations, Ur raised its head to heaven like a bull, Larsa the city beloved of Utu rejoiced, Umma the city beloved of Sara raised high its horn, the region of Zabala cried out like a ewe reunited with its lamb, and [some other city] raised its neck to the sky.

Lugalzagesi may have controlled only the half-dozen places specifically mentioned in this inscription, and some of those loosely. It is difficult to believe he reached the Mediterranean; this claim perhaps reflects nothing but some kind

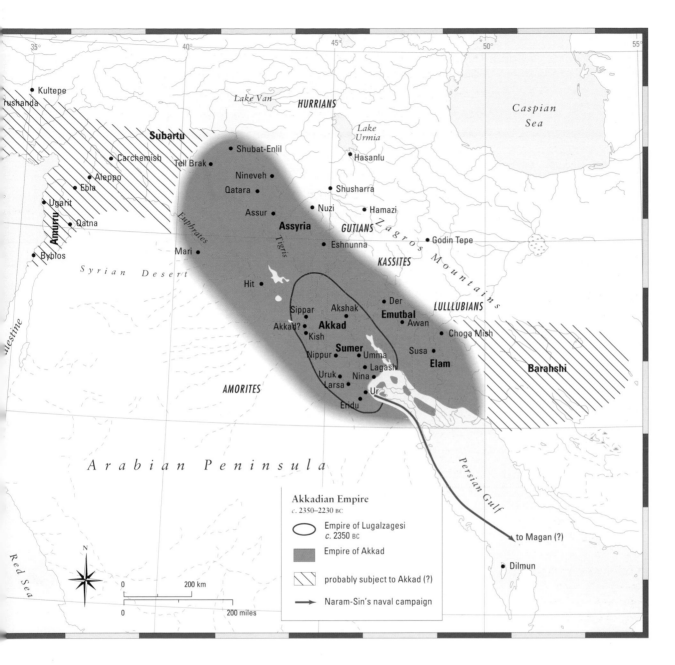

Akkadian Empire
c. 2350–2230 BC

Empire of Lugalzagesi
c. 2350 BC

Empire of Akkad

probably subject to Akkad (?)

Naram-Sin's naval campaign

of suzerainty over the city of Mari on the upper Euphrates, which was the western outpost of the Sumerian world, and which in turn may have had ties to Ebla and other towns in Syria. But Lugalzagesi clearly tried to turn the traditional *nam-lugal* primacy into a position of real power. He demonstrated his ability to sack cities and his willingness to despoil the temples of the gods. He began an escalation of warfare which soon buried him, for he was the unwitting teacher of Sargon of Akkad.

The name Sargon translates as 'legitimate king', which probably means he was not one. According to the *King List* he started out as a cupbearer to the king of Kish, but somehow became ruler of a new city called Akkad, which has never been found but was probably near Kish; and he is supposed to have reigned fifty-six years, but we do not know when or by what stages he built his empire. (The dates now commonly accepted for his reign are 2371–2316 BC, but as a reminder of the uncertainties of Bronze Age chronology it may be mentioned that some scholars have placed him a century earlier and others a century later.) He overthrew Lugalzagesi of Uruk, made himself king of Kish, Uruk and Ur, as well as Akkad, and placed 'men of Akkad' as *ensi* in other cities. His inscriptions declare:

Sargon, king of Kish, was victorious in 34 campaigns and dismantled [the walls of all] the cities, as far as the shore of the sea … Enlil did not let anyone oppose Sargon, the king. 5,400 soldiers ate daily in his palace.

The fragments of the Stele of Sargon show Akkadian soldiers taking prisoners after a revolt. This monument may belong to the reign of one of Sargon's sons, Rimush or Manishtushu, both of whom succeeded him in the kingship and had to suppress numerous revolts.

The exact extent of the Akkadian Empire is difficult to ascertain. According to Sargon's inscriptions he campaigned eastwards into Iran where he subjugated Elam, the ancient enemy of the Sumerians, and marched westwards up the Euphrates, taking Mari and Ebla, and reached the 'Cedar Forest' (Mount Lebanon). But an inscription of his grandson Naram-Sin claims this ruler was the *first* to take Ebla. Tablets in Akkadian, the Semitic dialect which was the official language of the empire (demonstrating some degree of control by Sargon or his successors), have been found at a score of sites. These are mostly in the Sumerian heartland, but there are some in the north, including Assur, the capital of the later Assyria, and some in Susa, the capital of Elam and later of Persia.

Bronze head of an Akkadian king, three-quarters life size. This probably represents Naram-Sin, Sargon's grandson, under whom the empire reached its apex of centralization. He left many more inscriptions than any other Akkadian king and was the first Mesopotamian ruler to deify himself.

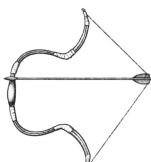

We also hear of expeditions to a place called Magan, located somewhere on the Persian Gulf.

The figure 5,400, a round number in a sexagesimal system of arithmetic, may include courtiers of all sorts, but Sargon's most pressing needs were military. There is evidence of a system of recruitment in which landholdings were granted in exchange for military service, like the 'feudal' customs of medieval Europe. In addition to this core army of 5,000 we may assume the availability of many thousands of conscripts drafted from royal and temple lands by the old methods, whose recruitment was the responsibility of the city governors. Both standing army and city troops were under the command of a general called the *sagina*; there was also a word that can be translated 'captain'. An army without much bureaucratic support must operate under severe logistical limitations; it can carry provisions for only three days, which means that the effective range of Sargon's army was 50 miles. From one or another of their major bases the Akkadian kings could reach most places in Mesopotamia and they effected the conquest of Elam in south-west Iran; their expeditions to Syria were presumably long-distance raids to acquire tribute.

Recurved,
COMPOSITE BOWS

Composite bows are made from different materials, usually wood, horn, and sinew, glued together. Great force is required to string such a bow but when strung it has enormous tension. Ancient examples may have had an extreme range of 180 yards. It is hard to tell simple from composite bows in artistic representations, so the date of its invention is disputed. But the expense of the weapon suggests it did not become common until c. 2300 BC.

The secret of Sargon's success was doubtless siegecraft. This was the advantage of his novel standing army, as sieges are extremely labour-intensive operations. Most of our information about siege warfare comes from the Mari tablets of the early second millennium, but it is reasonable to assume that advances in siegecraft we find there go back to the time of Sargon, the king who 'dismantled' the walls of the cities.

There seem to have been three major technological innovations. Firstly, there is frequent mention of a technique translated as 'sapping'. Since Mesopotamian walls were of brick, this probably did not mean digging under the walls in the fashion of medieval and early modern sappers, but rather digging *through* them. A wall-painting of the twentieth century BC found at Beni Hasan in Egypt provides our only good pictorial representation of the technique: three men, standing inside a sort of movable hut, are poking at a city wall with a long heavy beam, probably tipped with metal, which may be described as a primitive ram, though for levering rather than battering.

Secondly, the construction of earthen ramps beside city walls became an exact science. Babylonian texts from the second millennium have preserved

This fresco from the tomb of Khety, one of several tombs of provincial governors at Beni Hasan in Egypt, shows the besiegers of a well-fortified city using axes, composite bows, and a primitive ram. The upper registers are filled with wrestling scenes resembling modern unarmed combat manuals.

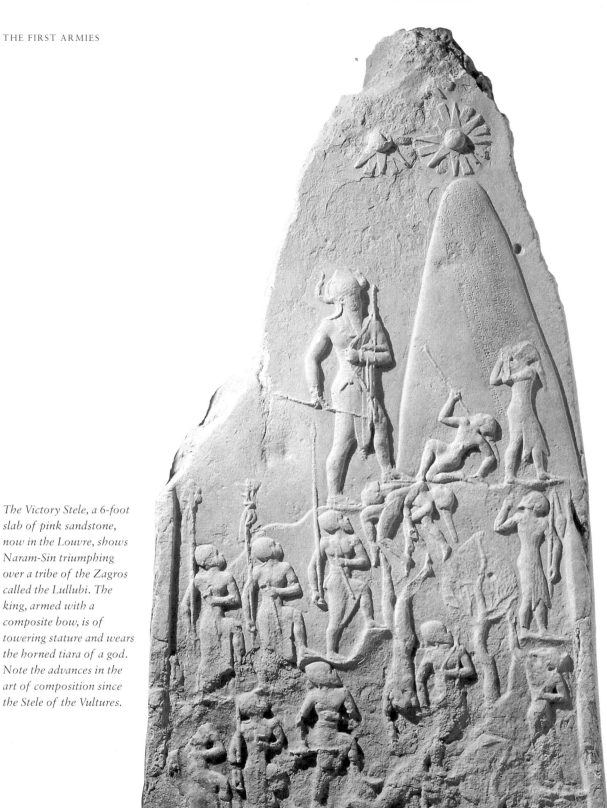

The Victory Stele, a 6-foot slab of pink sandstone, now in the Louvre, shows Naram-Sin triumphing over a tribe of the Zagros called the Lullubi. The king, armed with a composite bow, is of towering stature and wears the horned tiara of a god. Note the advances in the art of composition since the Stele of the Vultures.

mathematical exercises which show that engineers, if they knew the height of a wall, could calculate precisely the volume of earth, the number of men, and the time required to complete a ramp. According to these calculations, it would take 10,000 men only five days to build a ramp to the top of a wall 60 feet high. Such a ramp would have been worth its prodigious labour costs, for its completion spelled doom to a city. The final assault up the ramp in the face of the defenders' missiles would have been an unnerving moment, but once at the top the attackers could easily sweep off the defenders, who had no room on the battlements to form up in depth. And even a half-completed ramp would enable sappers to prise at the upper and thinner sections of the wall.

Finally, siege towers were in common use, probably as platforms for bowmen and slingers; and so was the composite bow, which roughly doubled the range and power of archery. A famous sculpture from the twenty-third century, the Victory Stele, shows Naram-Sin, grandson of Sargon, armed with what is generally agreed to be the earliest artistic representation of this deadly weapon. Without such firepower the new siegecraft might not have been practical, as it exposed the besiegers to constant fire from the walls. Now they could answer this with their own fire from towers at the same level as the battlements.

There were of course attempts to counter the new siegecraft with improvements in the art of fortification. In the Beni Hasan fresco the besieged fortress has battlements with crenellations and machicolated balconies to protect archers, and a glacis, or sloping bank, at the foot of the wall to keep off sappers. The most elaborate fortification so far discovered by archaeologists is the twentieth-century Egyptian fort at Buhen, now in Sudan: it had a double wall, bristling with towers, bastions and loopholes, surrounded by a deep ditch, and outside that a third wall with a glacis. Such a place must have been a hard nut to crack, but there can be little doubt that by Akkadian times walls were no longer invulnerable when faced with a besieger of sufficient determination and means.

The immense manpower required by the new siege warfare explains the success of the kingdom of Akkad, the first state in history that could draw not only upon a large standing army but on practically unlimited amounts of conscript labour. Every capture of a city replenished the labour pool; in the light of later Mesopotamian practices, we can assume that after the initial sack the survivors will have been deported into conditions of forced labour for the king, or for such nobles and temples as he chose to reward.

The Akkadian dynasty achieved the most impressive conquests and created the largest polity in history to that date. It gave Mesopotamia a permanent sense of cultural if not political unity: henceforth the land was called 'Sumer and Akkad', comprising the old Sumerian south and the newer Semitic north, and its two languages were called Sumerian and Akkadian.

Yet the Akkadian Empire was short-lived. Until the site and archives of Akkad are discovered we will not know how it was governed, but it seems likely that as a unit it was not governed at all. Akkadian governors may have been

THE SICKLE SWORD

The invention of bronze made possible the first swords. The common sword of the Bronze Age was the sickle sword, in Egypt called a khopesh from the Egyptian word for the foreleg of an animal. Never more than 18 inches long, it had only one edge and was used for slashing, not thrusting; hence the biblical phrase 'he smote with the edge of the sword'.

BABYLON UNDER THE DYNASTY OF HAMMURABI

Babylon is the best known of ancient Middle Eastern cities. The city uncovered by modern archaeologists is the one rebuilt by the Neo-Babylonian kings in the sixth century BC; the high water table has prevented deeper excavations. But the fragments of a description of Babylon written probably in the thirteenth century BC indicate the major buildings always occupied the same sites. This map attempts to reconstruct the original Babylon as it may have looked under the dynasty of Hammurabi (eighteenth to seventeenth centuries BC), to show Bronze Age fortification at its height. The city is seen from the north. The walls stretch a mile and a half from east to west. A processional way led from the Ishtar Gate to Eridu, the central district where the ziggurat and the temple of Marduk stood. The quay wall on the east bank of the Euphrates may not have been built until later.

Urash Gate

SUANNA

Temple of Ninurta

Temple of Ishhara

Zababa Gate

TE.EKI

Temple of Ashratum

Temple of Ishtar, Lady of Akkad

Temple of Nabû

Marduk Gate

KULLAB

NEWTOWN

Temple of the Mother Goddess

N

500 m

1/4 mile

Shamas Gate

TUBA

Adad Gate

E-Sangil,
Temple
of Marduk

Euphrates

King's Gate

ERIDU

KUMAR

Ziggurrat,
or temple-tower,
of Babylon

Enlil Gate

KA-DINGIRRA

Palace

Ishtar Gate

Euphrates

Babylon under the dynasty
of Hammurabi

appointed, but there is evidence that the traditional ruling families remained in control of most cities. Akkad probably did not interfere with them as long as they paid tribute and made no attempt to rebuild the city walls. The Akkadian 'empire' was a loose hegemonial structure, an unwilling federation held together by the standing army of five thousand men, the equivalent of a single Roman legion. Both of Sargon's sons had to reconquer it afresh and both died by assassination. His grandson Naram-Sin (reigned 2291–2255 BC), who called himself 'King of the Four Quarters' and 'God of Akkad', imposed more centralization. But the empire hardly outlived Naram-Sin's son, who was named Shar-Kali-Sharri (2255–2230 BC). In the reign of Shar-Kali-Sharri the frontiers began to be infiltrated by various barbarian peoples: mountaineers from the Zagros range called the Guti, Semitic tribes from Syria known to the Akkadians as 'Amorites' (westerners), and Hurrians from northern Mesopotamia. The anarchy of the last years of Akkad was such that at one point the compilers of the *King List* could only say 'Who was king? Who was not king?'.

FROM THE NILE TO THE INDUS

To most readers the ancient Middle East means primarily Egypt, and it may seem surprising to find the Nile valley treated so summarily here. But for its first millennium Egypt had practically no military history, this happy deficiency the result of an extraordinarily circumscribed geography, which imposed a precocious political unification upon the land while insulating it from external enemies.

Agricultural settlement on the Nile began about 5000 BC, as on the Euphrates. As the Sahara dried up, Neolithic farmers began to move into the flood plain of the great river, which once it was cleared of jungle provided the richest and easiest farming on earth. Their population grew rapidly and the increasingly forbidding desert hemmed them in. By the late fourth millennium there were long-distance trade connections with the Uruk civilization in Mesopotamia, and a complex culture began to evolve. But it was not based upon cities, and city states of the Sumerian type never developed. There appear to have been clusters of villages under local chieftains, corresponding to the nomes (the thirty-six territorial divisions) of pharaonic times, and these seem to have coalesced into states almost effortlessly; but there could never have been more than two or three kingdoms in the Nile valley, in contrast to the multiple independent centres that arose in Mesopotamia. According to an emphatic Egyptian tradition, the land had originally contained two kingdoms, Upper Egypt and Lower Egypt (the Delta), and had been united through the conquest of the Delta by the southern king; the memory of this division was preserved in the double crown of the pharaohs. This unification was without doubt effected through warfare. The Narmer Palette, deposited around 3100 BC in a temple on the upper Nile, shows a king wearing the crown of Upper Egypt killing an enemy with a mace, among other battle scenes. Both on the Nile and the Euphrates the rise of the state must have been accompanied by a flurry of intensive warfare. In

FLINT KNIFE

Scenes of war are frequent in early Egyptian art. This flint knife with carved ivory handle dates from the Predynastic period (3500–3100 BC).

On the Narmer Palette, a
2-foot-high slate palette for
grinding eye-paint, found
at Nekhen (Hierakonpolis),
a king of godlike stature
wearing the crown of
Upper Egypt brandishes a
mace while clutching an
enemy. On the upper right
Horus the falcon god
captures a prisoner from
the Delta (symbolized by
papyrus plants).

CEREMONIAL MACE

The Scorpion King, perhaps
a predecessor of Narmer,
is known only from
ceremonial maces found at
Nekhen, which show him
wearing the two crowns and
subduing enemies.

Mesopotamia this led to an age of fortification; in Egypt it resulted in unification so quickly that elaborate fortifications never arose and such as existed were pulled down by the pharaohs.

After unification there was slight need for any military function and pharaohs do not again appear in military scenes until the New Kingdom, fifteen centuries later. In the Old Kingdom or Pyramid Age (the Third to the Sixth Dynasties, 2686–2181 BC), there were indeed local disturbances, brigandage from

On the other side of the Narmer Palette a king wearing the crown of Lower Egypt, preceded by standard-bearers, visits a battlefield where ten corpses lie with heads between their legs. On each side the hieroglyphs for the name Narmer appear at the top between two images of Hathor the cow goddess.

THE INDUS VALLEY CIVILIZATION

The mysterious Indus Valley civilization, often called 'Harappan' after one of its two main centres (the other was Mohenjo-Daro), lasted for several centuries with little apparent change. The region was then much more fertile than now. There was a great dockyard at Lothal.

Berber nomads in the Libyan Desert and raids into the southern nomes by Nubian tribes. The pharaohs also had a degree of interest in the Levant, the only civilized region that touched their borders; Egyptian merchants kept up a flourishing trade with the port of Byblos to import Syrian wine and olive oil; there were occasional military expeditions into Palestine and cities were besieged and taken, but with no attempt at occupation. As we have seen, the most useful pictorial evidence for Early Bronze Age siege warfare comes from Egypt, thanks to the Egyptian custom of decorating tombs with detailed realistic paintings. Even the Old Kingdom could not do altogether without soldiers. But a society that could build the pyramids clearly had time on its hands.

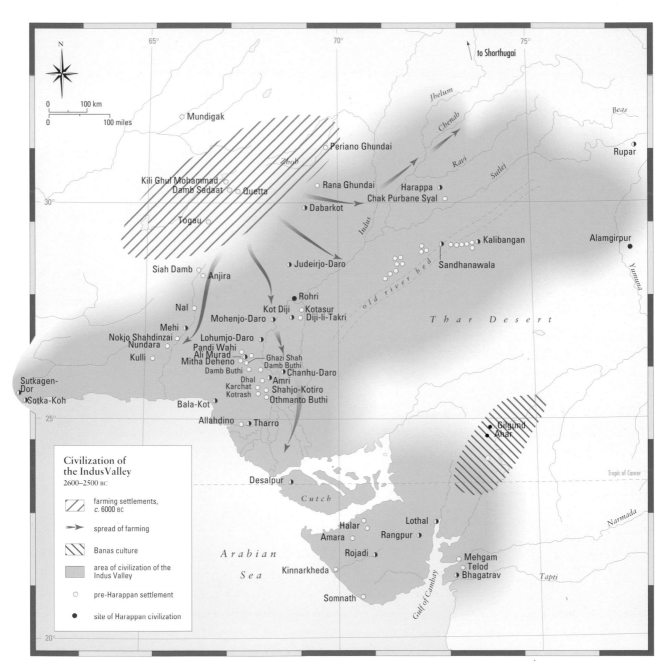

The third great riverine civilization of the Early Bronze Age remains an enigma. Agricultural settlement in the plain of the Indus River was as old as in Mesopotamia and Egypt. By the middle of the third millennium there had grown up there a complex culture with large cities, writing, massive architecture, long-distance trade networks and most of the other appurtenances of civilization. In geographical extent it was the largest civilization yet, stretching a thousand miles across what is now Pakistan and north-west India, with an offshoot as far away as Afghanistan. Superficially it looked much like the culture of Sumer, but there are also striking differences. In the cities of the Indus no imposing temples, palaces or royal tombs have yet been found; there are citadels but no massive fortifications, and no sign of serious warfare; tombs yield thousands of metal objects but no luxury goods. In other words, the archaeological relics of political centralization and steep social stratification, so familiar and unmistakable in the Middle East, are lacking here. For an Early Bronze Age civilization it seems oddly decentralized and unwarlike. It has been proposed that the states of the Indus were mercantile states, dependent on trade rather than territorial control. But they still seem highly organized, and it can only be speculated who organized and ran them because the Indus script has so far defied deciphering.

The Mesopotamian pattern of chronic interstate warfare, which, to judge from the evidence of fortification, appears to have spread quickly to the offshoots of Mesopotamian culture in Elam and Syria, was absent from both the Nile and the Indus throughout the Early Bronze Age. It failed to develop in Egypt because the civilization was too circumscribed, and possibly it never developed in India because that civilization, with its vast territory and widely spaced cities, was not circumscribed enough, although at present we have insuffient knowledge about it for there to be any certainty. In any case the Mesopotamian pattern was fated to become the pattern of the future, for civilizations could not remain isolated from one another forever.

THE END OF THE EARLY BRONZE AGE

The synchronic collapse of the Akkadian Empire and the Old Kingdom of Egypt is striking. The pharaonic regime at Memphis was already beginning to lose its grip on Egypt during the later years of Pepi II of the Sixth Dynasty, whose ninety-year reign (about 2275–2185 BC) was the longest in the history of the world. A few years after his death the Sixth Dynasty followed him. It was said there were seventy pharaohs at Memphis in seventy days. After 2160 BC there were none. There ensued a time of troubles known to Egyptologists as the First Intermediate Period (2181–2040 BC), when the Nile valley was divided among petty warring principalities, and invaders from Palestine raided and partly occupied the Delta. The increasing militarization of Egyptian society is reflected in the tomb paintings, where the peaceful domestic scenes of Old Kingdom art are replaced by portrayals of warlords surrounded by their armed retainers.

As we have seen, the Akkadian state was falling to pieces throughout the latter half of Pepi's reign, and vanished almost simultaneously with the Sixth Dynasty. There followed a century of disunity when much of the land between the Tigris and Euphrates was dominated by Gutian and other barbarian chieftains and the rest was divided among the resurgent city states. Then around 2113 BC (the chronology of this period is more than usually uncertain) Sumer and Akkad were reunited under the king of Ur. In the *Sumerian King List* this is labelled the Third Dynasty of Ur, but it was not a traditional *nam-lugal* primacy like the first

two dynasties of Ur, rather a genuine revival of the Sargonid Empire. Its extensive archives show that the regime exceeded the Akkadian state in administrative activity and greatly expanded the irrigation networks. The kings were routinely deified within their own lifetimes, following the example of the Akkadian Naram-Sin. But the empire of Ur III showed even less staying power than that of Akkad, lasting hardly more than a century. The northern and western frontiers were constantly threatened by the Amorites and other barbarians, against whom the kings of Ur erected massive fortifications: first an earthwork

The Third Dynasty of Ur, most centralized of ancient Mesopotamian empires, carried out a large building programme, including the ziggurat of the moon god at Ur, built by Ur-Nammu. The appearance of the its upper stages is uncertain.

across the narrow waist of the Tigris–Euphrates valley to the north of Kish, then an earthen 'Amorite wall' stretching 170 miles across the west. The final blow was delivered by an ancient civilized enemy, the Elamites from the south-east, who sacked Ur in about 2006 BC, plunging Mesopotamia back into political fragmentation and warfare.

Although our focus is on the rise and fall of empires, most city rulers in the Early Bronze Age were more interested in displaying their piety than their conquests. The votive plaques of Ur-Nanshe of Lagash, grandfather of Eanatum (see page 80), show him digging irrigation works, building temples, and surrounded by his family.

In Palestine and Syria city life was in decline through the last third of the millennium. There is considerable evidence of warfare and sack. The Egyptians were certainly responsible for some of this. About 2300 BC a Sixth Dynasty official named Uni recorded his military exploits on his tomb inscription: he had led no fewer than six expeditions into Palestine with armies recruited from all over Egypt, including Nubian and Libyan mercenaries; he had destroyed the walls of cities, slaughtered the inhabitants and laid waste their vines and fig (olive?) trees. As vineyards and groves are practically indestructible the threat to agriculture was mostly symbolic, but the threat to city walls was real. Over the next century or so, Ebla and Byblos were destroyed, trade with Egypt was cut off and urban life virtually disappeared, the population reverting to village

Mohenjo-Daro, greatest city of the Indus, was completely abandoned by the eighteenth century BC. There is evidence of violence, but the date seems too early for the destruction to be blamed on the Aryan invaders (for whom see the next chapter). Environmental factors such as changes in the course of the Indus may have played a part.

agriculture. Much of this devastation could have been the work of the Akkadians. But much else can be attributed to the Amorite nomads who were moving both east and west from their homeland in the Syrian Desert.

The wave of destruction extended, however, to places that should have been beyond the reach of Amorite or Akkadian. Around this time the great citadel of Troy in Anatolia (labelled Troy II by archaeologists), one of the most impressive fortifications in the Early Bronze Age world, went up in flames. Other towns vanished all around the Aegean. The Indus valley was in decline from 2200 BC; by 1800 BC its major city at Mohenjo-Daro in Pakistan was deserted; by 1500 BC the entire civilization had disappeared from history, for even its existence was forgotten until archaeologists discovered its ruins in the twentieth century AD.

AN AMORITE DAGGER

*An Amorite dagger with a
carved ivory handle from a
temple at Byblos in Syria.
These straight bronze blades
were for thrusting, not
slashing, and were not long
enough to be called true
swords. The only slashing
sword of the Bronze Age
was the not very effective
khopesh, illustrated on
page. 97. To us the word
'sword' usually means a
long cut-and-thrust weapon.
This type of sword, with a
bronze (later iron) blade
28 inches or more in length,
was invented in Europe
c. 1400 BC and did not
become common in the
Mediterranean until
c. 1200 BC (see endpapers).*

Despite the many chronological uncertainties, it now seems certain that about 2200 BC there began a prolonged worldwide crisis that eventually brought down all the high civilizations of the Early Bronze Age and ravaged their hinterlands. The nature of that crisis is still unclear. It has been suggested that the ultimate cause was sweeping environmental deterioration. The systematic study of climate change in antiquity is only just beginning, but there is mounting evidence that between 2200 and 1900 BC severe drought affected all of northern Africa, western Asia and much of Europe. In northern Mesopotamia throughout this period arable land was turning to desert and its inhabitants to pastoralism. This may have brought about the early demise of the Akkadian Empire, and may also have aborted the Third Dynasty of Ur. The kings of Ur never re-established control over the northern plain, the land later known as Assyria, presumably because that had become a land of nomads. This meant that Sumer and Akkad, only a century after its unification, was deprived of a large share of its territory and resources. The heartland of both dynasties lay in the south, but the agriculture of the south would have suffered also from the reduced flow of the Euphrates. An even worse problem was the population displacement created by the long drought in the north. This surely explains the recurrent migration of nomadic or semi-nomadic tribes into southern Mesopotamia from the north and west, beginning in the late twenty-third century. The expensive irrigation and fortification projects into which the Dynasty of Ur poured its resources were not signs of strength and prosperity; they look more like desperate and doomed efforts to cope with problems that had become insoluble. Egypt at the beginning of the First Intermediate Period was likewise afflicted by a series of low Niles caused by drought in central Africa. A similar decrease in the flow of the Indus may have caused the decline of Indian civilization.

From the available evidence, however, it does not seem that the crisis was accompanied by obvious environmental problems everywhere. On the Mediterranean coastlands, whose economies were not based on rivers, the problems seem to have been more political and military than environmental. Nor did political and environmental stress always synchronize. Therefore it seems worth suggesting that another cause of the world crisis was the escalation of warfare begun by Sargon of Akkad. The Akkadian kings developed two deadly innovations, systematic siegecraft and the composite bow, which made warfare far more destructive to human communities. Sargon and his successors carried the new warfare to the Mediterranean and probably initiated the mounting violence that within two centuries practically obliterated urban civilization in Syria and Palestine. The Sixth Dynasty campaigns in Palestine may be interpreted as a response to the growing instability in that region. A century later the turmoil engulfed Egypt itself, and then spread havoc around the Aegean. The end of the Indus culture, however, is still too obscure to enable us to say how it may fit into this picture.

The earliest states must have been highly vulnerable to total systems collapse under stress. Simpler societies can deal with intolerable pressures by dispersal. But when complex agrarian societies were subjected to unaccustomed challenges, such as external enemies or environmental deterioration, they could only respond by increasing their bureaucratic and military establishments. The problem with this is that after a certain point, increased socio-political complexity in a technologically primitive world has to produce a diminishing rate of return: once the cheap solutions have been used up, complexity becomes increasingly expensive, and more and more must be spent simply to maintain the status quo. The Third Dynasty of Ur invested heavily in irrigation, but the suddenness of its collapse suggests it was exploiting marginal land that was hardly worth the effort. Most states after 2300 BC found themselves involved in an arms race that required immense expenditure on standing armies, siege trains, and fortifications, yet brought none of the rewards that Sargon had reaped because now all states had armies like that. The state became top-heavy, its burdens too great for an exploited population to bear; eventually local units opted for independence and the system collapsed under its own weight. The fall of the Early Bronze Age civilizations may have been the first demonstration of a pattern that would repeat itself throughout ancient and medieval history. For example, the collapse of the Western Roman Empire in the fifth century AD has been explained in the same general terms. But the first civilizations, with their relatively weak economic and technical base, may have been particularly fragile.

THE MIDDLE BRONZE AGE RECOVERY

Nothing halted the decline of urban civilization in India, but in the Middle East the dawn of the second millennium brought social and economic revival and inaugurated the generally prosperous and stable period known to archaeologists as the Middle Bronze Age. The signs of recovery are clearest in Egypt, where the rulers of Thebes reunited the land and established what is called the Middle Kingdom (Eleventh and Twelfth Dynasties, 2040–1786 BC). In the Intermediate Period there had been Semitic raiders in the Delta in addition to the general insecurity; hence the pharaohs of the Middle Kingdom, though determined to keep Egypt in splendid isolation, were obliged to pay more attention to military affairs and to the frontiers than did their predecessors. A sizeable standing army was maintained, including many Nubian and Berber mercenaries, and was armed with bronze weapons, which for the first time became common in Egypt. The Nile valley has two vulnerable points of entry, at its northern end and its southern end; both were firmly plugged. The southern frontier advanced to the Second Cataract, and to guard it from the Nubians a chain of forts stretched 250 miles up

These wooden model soldiers, found in the tomb of Mesehti, a provincial governor of the Eleventh Dynasty (twentieth century BC), are an important source for Egyptian weaponry. They include forty Egyptian spearmen with wooden shields (shown here) and forty Nubian archers with simple bows.

the Nile, including the great stronghold at Buhen; this has been called the first deliberately planned system of strategic territorial defence in history. On the northern frontier the Sinai peninsula was fortified and occasional raids were made into Palestine, probably to maintain an Egyptian sphere of influence there.

In Mesopotamia the drought in the north finally ended and population and wealth recovered. The barbarian invaders were soon assimilated and many cities acquired Amorite or Hurrian dynasties. But the age of genuinely independent city states was over; from now on a small city could survive only as an ally of a hegemonic city, and the power of a leading city was judged by the number of its client states. Between 2000 and 1800 BC a rough balance of power prevailed

among the four strongest cities, each with its ring of dependants: the south was dominated by Isin and Larsa, the north by Assur and Eshnunna. In addition two powerful Amorite cities in northern Syria, Yamhad and Qatna, were involved in Mesopotamian affairs. It happens that most of our detailed information about interstate relations in Mesopotamia comes from this period, owing to the discovery at Mari of a cache of thousands of tablets, including much diplomatic correspondence. One of these letters summarizes the political situation of the early eighteenth century BC in terms recognizable to diplomats of any age:

> There is no king who is strong on his own: Hammurapi [Hammurabi] of Babylon has a following of 10 or 15 kings, Rim-Sin of Larsa the same, Ibal-pi-El of Esnunna [Eshnunna] the same, Amut-pi-El of Qatna the same, and Yarim-Lim of Yamhad has a following of 20 kings.

The reconstruction of Early Bronze Age warfare attempted earlier in this chapter was based largely on the evidence of the Mari archives, as there seems no

MIDDLE EAST 2000 BC

By 2000 BC the Egyptians have turned lower Nubia (Wawat) into a province and established a Red Sea port at Sawu for trade with east Africa; the empire of Ur III is approaching collapse; and records of Assyrian merchants show central Anatolia is already occupied by the later Hittites.

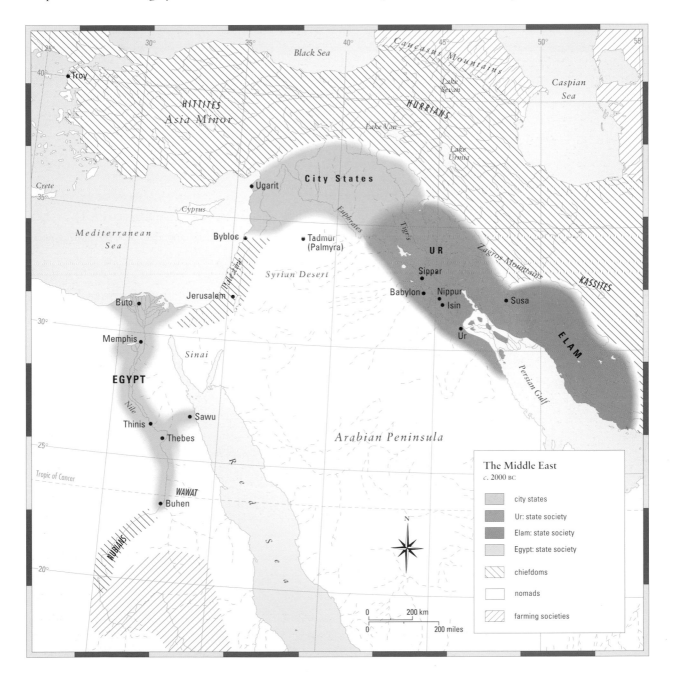

The Middle East
c. 2000 BC

- city states
- Ur: state society
- Elam: state society
- Egypt: state society
- chiefdoms
- nomads
- farming societies

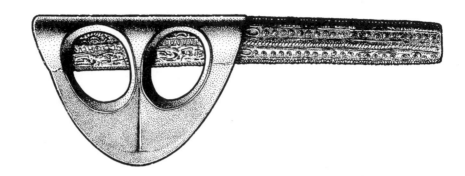

Maces continued in use as ceremonial weapons but the invention of bronze made possible the true axe, the preferred hand-to-hand weapon of the Bronze Age. This type of battleaxe, called an 'eye axe' by archaeologists, was used in Egypt and the Levant during the Middle Bronze Age. The bronze blade is attached to the haft by three tangs. In Mesopotamia an axe with a narrow chisel-like blade was favoured; examples of this can be seen on the Stele of the Vultures.

reason to suppose that much change in military tactics or equipment had taken place. The letters reveal a network of inter-city alliances that sometimes stretched all across Mesopotamia and Syria, and some campaigns, suggesting a level of logistical support comparable to that of the High Bronze Age, which we will look at in the next chapter. The above-mentioned Yarim-Lim, king of Yamhad, whose capital was at Aleppo, wrote as follows complaining of the ingratitude of Yashub-Yahad, king of Der (east of the Tigris), who was also an Amorite prince and an old ally:

> May Samas [Shamash, god of justice] investigate my conduct and yours, and render judgement! I behave to you like a father and brother and you behave to me like an ill-wisher and enemy. What requital is this for the fact that the weapons of Adad and Yarim-Lim rescued the city of Babylon, and gave life to your land and yourself?
>
> Had it not been for Adad and Yarim-Lim the city of Der would have been blown away like chaff 15 years ago, so that one would be unable to find it and you would not be able to act like this. Indeed, Sin-Gamil, the King of Diniktum [a port on the Tigris], like you is rewarding me with hostility and obstructions. I have moored 500 boats in the quay of Diniktum, and for twelve years I have supported his land and himself. Now you are rewarding me with hostility and obstructions like him.
>
> I swear to you by Addu [Adad], the god of my city, and Sin my personal god, I shall not rest until I have destroyed your land and yourself! Now I shall come at the beginning of spring, and I shall advance to the doors of your city gate, and shall acquaint you with the bitterness of the weapons of Adad and Yarim-Lim.

The documents often mention armies numbering 10,000 men; once we hear of 20,000 and once of 30,000. They often speak of engagements; kings are always being 'opposed by weapons' and claiming glorious victories. About 1800 Shamshi-Adad I, king of Assur, wrote to his son:

> You think up stratagems to beat the enemy and to manoeuvre for position against him. But the enemy will likewise try to think up

stratagems and to manoeuvre for position against you, just as two wrestlers use tricks against each other.

The advice sounds timeless, but the kind of warfare Shamshi-Adad probably had in mind was that of his own time. The documents tell us nothing about what happened when armies met in the open field, but they tell us much about sieges, and the stratagems the king meant were primarily diplomatic manoeuvres to assemble enough allies to carry out or relieve a siege. When the king of Mari was attacked by three allied kings, he called on his patron the king of Yamhad for help; but instead of challenging the three kings to a pitched battle they besieged them in their stronghold and 'destroyed their ramparts'. Warfare in the Middle Bronze Age seems to mean siege warfare, as it probably had been since the city walls arose. Shamshi-Adad once mobilized 60,000 men for a siege. Sieges use all

Hammurabi of Babylon (1792–1750 BC), here raising his arm in worship, did not assemble his empire until toward the end of his reign. In about 1760 BC he began a series of diplomatic and military manoeuvres to achieve hegemony over Mesopotamia, defeating and absorbing in turn the powerful cities of Larsa, Eshnunna, and Mari.

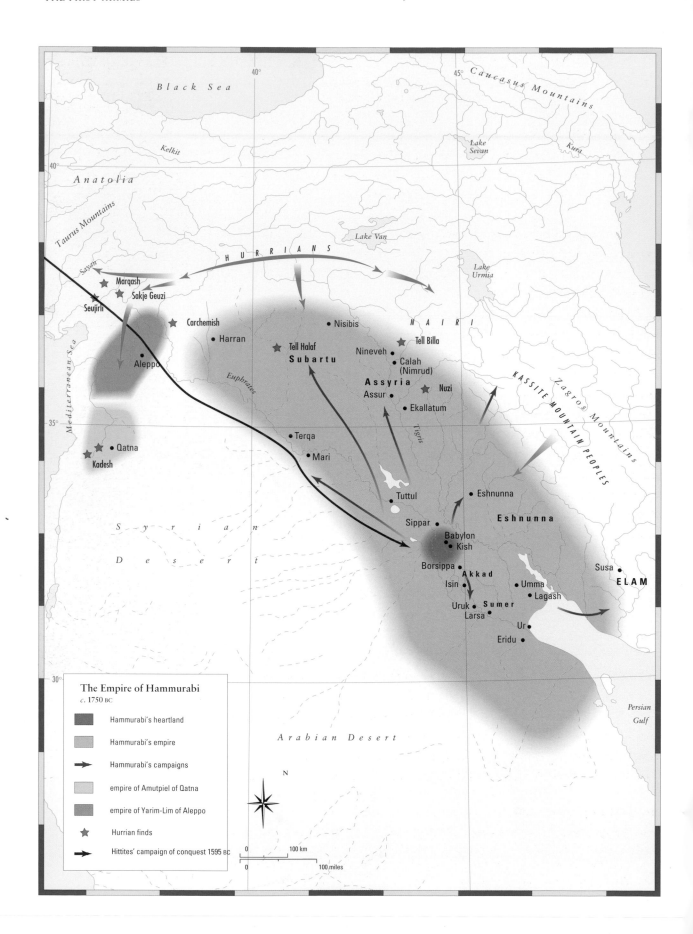

The Empire of Hammurabi
c. 1750 BC

Hammurabi's heartland

Hammurabi's empire

Hammurabi's campaigns

empire of Amutpiel of Qatna

empire of Yarim-Lim of Aleppo

Hurrian finds

Hittites' campaign of conquest 1595 BC

Black Sea

Caucasus Mountains

Kelkit

Lake Sevan

Kura

Anatolia

Taurus Mountains

Lake Van

H U R R I A N S

Saym

Marqash

Sakje Geuzi

Seujirli

Carchemish

Harran

Lake Urmia

Nisibis

N A I R I

Tell Halaf

Subartu

Nineveh

Tell Billa

Mediterranean Sea

Aleppo

Calah (Nimrud)

Assyria

Assur

Nuzi

Euphrates

Ekallatum

KASSITE MOUNTAIN PEOPLES

Zagros Mountains

Terqa

Mari

Tigris

Qatna

Kadesh

Tuttul

S y r i a n

Eshnunna

D e s e r t

Sippar

Eshnunna

Babylon

Kish

Susa

Borsippa

ELAM

Akkad

Isin

Umma

Lagash

Uruk

Sumer

Larsa

Ur

Eridu

Arabian Desert

Persian Gulf

N

0   100 km

0   100 miles

the methods described above – rams, towers, ramps – and often with deadly effect; we hear of cities that fell in a week or even in a single day. But many did not. A garrison commander wrote to the king of Eshnunna:

> Say to my lord: The troops are well. The city is safe. The garrison of my lord is strong. Even if the Amorites should make war for ten years and bring ten battering rams, ten siege towers and twenty ladders(?), I will remain strong in my city. My lord should not worry.

The fact that the balance of power lasted so long suggests that warfare was normally limited and indecisive. A game restricted to defensive strategies must end in stalemate unless one of the players can assemble an overwhelming coalition.

The balance was eventually upset by a new player, the city of Babylon near Kish. Babylon was never a place of any importance until the nineteenth century BC, when it came under the rule of an ambitious Amorite dynasty. Under its able king Hammurabi (reigned 1792–1750 BC) it quickly rose to become the leading power in Mesopotamia and created an empire nearly as extensive as the empire of Akkad at its height. Hammurabi is remembered for his law code and for the other products of the Babylonian literary and artistic efflorescence that distinguished his reign; it was then that Babylon became the religious and cultural capital of Mesopotamia, a position it was to keep for the next fifteen centuries. But the Babylonian Empire, even by Mesopotamian standards, was an ephemeral political structure, lasting only a few years: it was not completed until nearly the end of Hammurabi's life, and began to fall apart soon after his death. By 1700 BC Mesopotamia had reverted to the normal fractiousness which most of its rulers clearly found congenial. The same arts of siegecraft that had made it easy to unify the land in the days of Sargon, once they were widely disseminated, made it impossible to unify thereafter.

Certain factors remained constant throughout the millennium and a half surveyed in this chapter. Civilization in the Early and Middle Bronze Age remained an obstinately parochial affair, based on the two ancient centres of the Nile and Tigris–Euphrates valleys, each pursuing its independent destiny. The copious records of Mesopotamia in the time of Hammurabi do not contain a single mention of Egypt; the Egyptians still knew almost nothing and cared less about the world beyond Palestine. But all that was about to change.

THE EMPIRE OF HAMMURABI

In his last years Hammurabi ruled an empire comparable to those of Akkad and Ur. His western frontier reached to the kingdom of Yamhad (Aleppo). Under his son the empire began to shrink, but Babylon remained a considerable power till the Hittite sack of 1595 BC. The Hurrians seem to have been increasing in numbers in northern Mesopotamia and Syria at this period but their movements are obscure.

The Code of Hammurabi is inscribed on an 8-foot stele, showing Hammurabi before Shamash, god of justice. The 282 laws are an eclectic sample and the purpose of the monument is unclear. It was put up at the very end of Hammurabi's life and may have been meant to advertise his role as dispenser of justice.

CHAPTER FOUR

The Wars of the Great Kingdoms 1700–1100 BC

DETAIL FROM THE EGYPTIAN RELIEFS commemorating the battle of Kadesh, 1275 BC. Ramesses II, protected by Nekhbet the vulture goddess, fires arrows from his racing chariot. Chariot warfare militarized society and created a new warrior aristocracy. Earlier rulers advertised their piety, but in the Late or High Bronze Age (1700–1100 BC) kings celebrated their military exploits above all else. The inscription describes Ramesses as 'great of victory over all foreign countries, one knows not when he will begin to fight; a strong wall about his army, their shield on the day of fighting; a bowman without his like ...'

THE WARS OF THE GREAT KINGDOMS

THE RISE OF CHARIOT WARFARE

In the late eighteenth century BC both the Egyptian Middle Kingdom and the Babylonian Empire fell apart. Everywhere records failed, leaving the seventeenth and much of the sixteenth century a dark age. In the old centres of civilization alien conquerors took over, and new powers arose in the north. Amorite and Hurrian invaders, called by the Egyptians *hyksos* ('foreign chieftains'), established themselves in the Nile Delta and in about 1650 BC proclaimed a new dynasty with its capital at Avaris – the first non-Egyptian dynasty in the history of Egypt. At about the same time a Hittite king called Hattusilis created a powerful state, controlling central Anatolia from his citadel at Hattusas. His successor Mursilis extended Hittite rule over northern Syria, and in 1595 BC performed the most spectacular military exploit in history to that date, when he led his army all the way to Mesopotamia, sacked the great city of Babylon and carried off the statue of its god Marduk, doubtless accompanied by much booty of a secular nature. As a result, the enfeebled dynasty of Hammurabi vanished

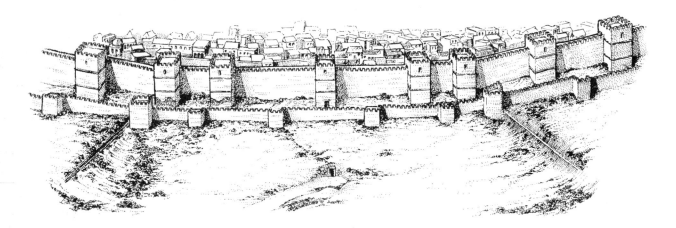

HATTUSAS, NEAR MODERN BOGHAŽKOY, TURKEY

The best example of city fortification in the High Bronze Age. The citadel was built on a rocky outcrop dominating the surrounding plateau. The upper parts of walls have not survived, but can be reconstructed with the aid of Egyptian art. The postern in the foreground led to a tunnel under the wall used for sorties.

and was soon replaced by barbarians known as Kassites from the Iranian hills. Like earlier barbarian invaders of Mesopotamia they were quickly Akkadianized; their king called himself 'King of the Kassites', but also 'King of Sumer and Akkad'; and the dynasty lasted longer than any of the native dynasties of Sumer and Akkad, though next to nothing is known of its history. The Hurrian princes took advantage of the general disorder: in about 1550 BC a great Hurrian kingdom called Mitanni arose in northern Mesopotamia and soon contested the domination of Syria with the Hittites.

All these kingdoms relied upon a new military technology, the horsed chariot and the composite bow. Early evidence for chariot warfare links it to the Hittite kingdom. The *hyksos* princes introduced it to Egypt, and then it became common all over the Middle East. But it is unlikely that the Hittites invented it. There is a mysterious but definite connection between chariot warfare and people of Aryan heritage, that is, speaking dialects ancestral to the Aryan or Indo-Iranic division of the Indo-European linguistic family. Today Aryan languages are spoken in Iran, much of Central Asia and most of the Indian subcontinent. The oldest literary evidence for an Aryan language is the collection of Sanskrit hymns called the *Rig-Veda*, composed in about 1500 BC. Most of the people of the kingdom of Mitanni spoke Hurrian, but the aristocracy, all chariot warriors, had Aryan names and worshipped the same gods – Indra, Varuna, Mithra – who appear in the *Rig-Veda*. Many cities in Syria and Palestine acquired dynasties with Aryan or Hurrian names at this time. Some scholars have thought that even the Kassites of Babylonia (whose original language is obscure, but could not have been Indo-European) paid homage to some Aryan gods. Everywhere the Aryan word *maryannu* (young warrior) was used for chariot fighters. There survives a Hittite treatise on the training of chariot horses, translated from Hurrian, which is studded with Aryan technical terms. In the fourteenth century, when this treatise was written, Aryan may no longer have been spoken in the Middle East, but it was still the international language of chariotry, as Italian is of music.

It is widely supposed that the ancestors of these Aryans had come from the

The King's Gate of Hattusas, viewed from the inside looking out. This was originally a vaulted passage between two towers, which formed a citadel connecting the inner and outer walls. The gate was reached by a ramp exposed to fire from the towers. On the inner jamb Teshub the storm god guards the door with his battleaxe.

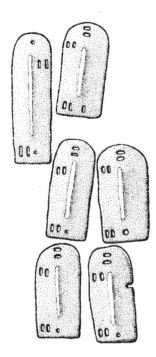

BRONZE ARMOUR SCALES
FROM HATTUSAS

*Body armour was invented
for chariotry, as charioteers
needed both hands and
could make little use of
shields. In all languages the
corselet was called by the
same Hurrian word. It
consisted of a leather tunic
sewn with hundreds of
metal scales, each about
3 inches long; the whole
garment weighed 12 pounds.
Probably both archer and
driver wore corselets, and
also helmets. Hittite chariot
crews added a third man as
shield bearer.*

north, and likewise the horse and the war chariot. The dissemination of the horse preceded the other two. The original range of the wild horse (*Equus caballus*) lay on the Eurasian steppe, where domesticated horses were being ridden as early as the fourth millennium BC. By 3000 BC there had developed a nomadic pastoral culture exploiting the deep steppe with riding horses and ox-drawn wheeled carts, stretching across the European steppe from the Dneister to the Ural River, and soon to spread across the steppes of Central Asia. Horse nomadism was never suitable for the arid steppes of the Middle East, but by the Middle Bronze Age Syrian and Mesopotamian princes were importing horses from the north and occasionally riding in horse-drawn chariots. These were prestige vehicles, with no military function.

The war chariot of the High Bronze Age was a much more specialized vehicle and could not have come from the European steppes, which lack the necessary woods. Many scholars think the likeliest place for its invention lies in the mountainous regions south of the Caucasus, where the high pastures were famous for horse-breeding in antiquity. Some think that we should also look there for the homeland of the Aryans. It seems certain that by around 1700 BC horsemen in that part of the world developed a chariot built of lightweight hardwoods, with two spoked wheels and a leather-mesh platform on which a rider could stand, the whole thing light enough (about 60 pounds) for one man to carry, and pulled by two fast horses. It was the first effective use of the horse as a draft animal, and the swiftest vehicle ever designed. It was surely invented for hunting, which always remained one of its main uses, but some enterprising highland chieftain soon experimented with using such chariots in war: that is, as a galloping archery platform, carrying two athletic young men, one an expert driver and the other an expert archer armed with a composite bow, firing a steady stream of arrows with a range of several hundred feet. The basic principle of the composite bow had been known in the Middle East for some centuries, but it was an expensive weapon requiring years to manufacture; like the rifle of the eighteenth century AD, it was probably used for hunting by kings and nobles, and in war by certain highly trained specialists. The weapon may not have been perfected, nor its full military potential realized, until it was mounted on a mobile platform. These inventions eventually spun off a third invention, the first real body armour: the archer, and sometimes the horses, were protected by leather tunics sewn with bronze or copper scales.

It has been suggested that chariot warfare was first tested early in the seventeenth century at Troy, which at that time was taken over by the conquerors who built the citadel known to archaeologists as Troy VI. Knowledge of the new art had spread far by about 1650 BC, when upstart regimes in Anatolia and Egypt used it in their rise to power. The long Hittite march to Babylon in 1595 BC demonstrated its full potential. Over the next century Aryan and Hurrian adventurers seized power in cities all around the Fertile Crescent.

These conquests were not mass migrations; rather, we should imagine quick takeovers by small military élites, resembling the Norman conquests of England and Sicily in the eleventh century AD. There was relatively little destruction; the transition from Middle to High Bronze Age was not marked by any general decline in material civilization, such as had accompanied the transition from Early to Middle Bronze Age. Like the medieval Norman knights, the chariot conquerors were soon absorbed culturally by the conquered. Only in two places did these conquests lead to lasting cultural and linguistic change. In the west, around 1600 BC, a band of Indo-European (but not Aryan) charioteers established themselves in Greece, and two centuries after that took over the more advanced Minoan civilization on Crete, adapting the linear Cretan script to write a language that was turning into Greek. In the east, a larger migration spread over the Iranian plateau and during the latter half of the second millennium overran northern India, taking over the remnants of the Indus River civilization, whose people became the lower castes of Hinduism; the oral poetry of the conquerors preserved faithfully an Aryan dialect that was turning into Sanskrit. But in the Middle East the upheavals were over by about 1550 BC, when the native Eighteenth Dynasty expelled the *hyksos* from Egypt. By that time the barbarians had been assimilated and a new pattern of interstate affairs had taken shape.

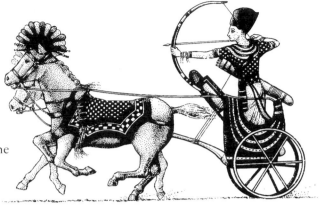

WAR CHARIOT

The war chariot was made possible by two inventions, the spoked wheel and the bit. Complete chariots have been found in Egyptian tombs. The frame was made of wood covered with leather. It had two wheels, each with four (later six) spokes, and an axle placed at the very rear of the body for stability on fast turns. Attached to the sides were one or two quivers, each containing thirty or forty arrows, a bow case, and sometimes a quiver for javelins.

INTERSTATE RELATIONS IN THE HIGH BRONZE AGE

The later Bronze Age, especially the fifteenth to the thirteenth centuries BC, has been described as 'the first international civilization' because what we usually mean by diplomacy and foreign affairs first became visible then. Something like this pattern had existed earlier, but on a far more localized scale, and, except for the Mari tablets, insufficiently documented. But after 1500 BC there was a constellation of powers in the known world, in constant contact with one another. Roads were busy with couriers carrying tablets in Akkadian (now the diplomatic language) in which kings exchanged flowery compliments, proposals of alliance and threats of war; after them came embassies burdened with sumptuous gifts and escorting princesses to be given in marriage; and occasionally huge armies were somewhere on the move, marching for days or weeks on end in columns that stretched for miles, obscuring the summer skies with the dust clouds raised by thousands of horsed chariots.

Normally there were three first-rank powers in that world. They called themselves the 'Great Kingdoms'. (Any king who ruled other kings was recognized as a Great King.) About 1550 BC the Eighteenth Dynasty at Thebes reunited all Egypt for the first time in two hundred years, and founded what we call the New Kingdom. It attempted a faithful restoration of the old pharaonic system in every respect but foreign policy, for it was now obvious that Egypt needed an aggressive one. The Nubian frontier was extended south to the Fourth

MIDDLE EAST
1500—1100 BC

Arzawa was a Luwian kingdom in western Anatolia intermittently subject to the Hittites. Somewhere further west and outside Hittite control lay a land known to the Hittites as Ahhiyawa, which is perhaps to be identified with the Achaeans (Mycenaean Greeks).

Cataract, well within the present Republic of Sudan, and many campaigns were waged to maintain an Egyptian sphere in the Levant as far north as the Euphrates. The Great Kingdom of Mitanni in northern Mesopotamia arose at the same time as the Egyptian New Kingdom. They were the two aggressive chariot states of the fifteenth century, and Syria was their battleground. But in the late fourteenth century the Mitannians were pushed out of Syria by the resurgent Hittite power, and in Mesopotamia they were soon overshadowed by the ascendancy of Assyria. It will be recalled that the Hittite state – the Great Kingdom of Hatti – had enjoyed a burst of glory during the time of troubles, which it may have initiated. It fell into eclipse during the fifteenth century, but in the fourteenth it recovered and replaced Mitanni as Egypt's rival for the

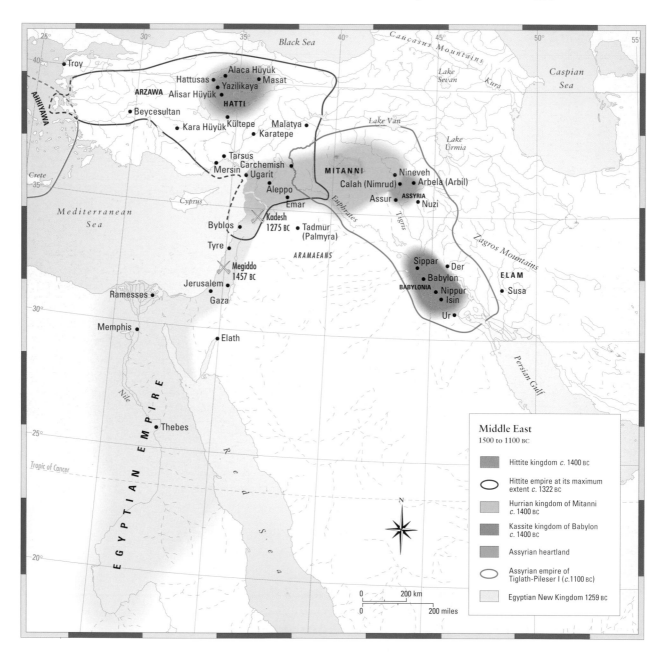

Middle East
1500 to 1100 BC

Hittite kingdom *c.* 1400 BC

Hittite empire at its maximum extent *c.* 1322 BC

Hurrian kingdom of Mitanni *c.* 1400 BC

Kassite kingdom of Babylon *c.* 1400 BC

Assyrian heartland

Assyrian empire of Tiglath-Pileser I (*c.*1100 BC)

Egyptian New Kingdom 1259 BC

control of Syria, which the two powers divided by treaty after the battle of Kadesh in 1275 BC.

To the east lay two kingdoms that were not as great. The Assyrian kingdom rose to unite northern Mesopotamia after 1350 BC, and the Kassite dynasty at Babylon continued to dominate the south. The two were perpetual rivals within Mesopotamia but had few ambitions outside it. The Levant, cockpit of the High Bronze Age, was a patchwork of small city states and tribes. The pharaoh Thutmose III claimed that at the battle of Megiddo he fought a coalition of no fewer than 330 Levantine princes. Some of these were to have their day in the future (in the late thirteenth century the pharaoh Merneptah celebrated in an inscription, among more significant victories in Palestine, his destruction of a

The outdoor sanctuary at Yazilikaya near Hattusas, a natural outcrop of rock covered with high reliefs, is the outstanding monument of Hittite religion. The sculptures show 'the thousand gods of Hatti' in procession. Male gods, shown below, wear fluted conical helmets and carry sickle swords; goddesses wear crowns.

tribal confederacy known as 'Israel'), but for now they were pawns of the Great Kings. More fortunate were the city states of Mycenaean Greece, which enjoyed a bustling trade with the east, enabling its charioteer princes to live in an opulent High Bronze Age style: the shaft graves at Mycenae contained more gold than has ever been found at any other archaeological site, and the palace at Cnossus on Crete may have been the largest in the world, but they were far enough from the

Egyptian infantry of the New Kingdom march in front of chariots. Their shields are strapped to their backs and they carry khopesh and axe, but are unarmoured. The Egyptian Army was organized in divisions of 5,000 men, named after gods who were probably the patrons of the recruitment districts.

CEREMONIAL AXE

Ceremonial axe of Queen Ahhotop given to her by her son the pharaoh Ahmose, founder of the Eighteenth Dynasty. Real battleaxes of the New Kingdom resembled this, with wide-edged blades designed to pierce armour.

crossroads of the Great Kingdoms to escape becoming their pawns. The Aryan charioteers, then engaged in the conquest of north India, had drifted entirely out of touch with Middle Eastern politics.

Egypt was the best-organized of the Great Kingdoms. The new Egyptian empire in the Levant rested on a firm Palestinian core of cities under resident Egyptian governors; beyond that, a zone of tributary allied cities stretched north to Ugarit; beyond that a more uncertain and fluctuating sphere of Egyptian influence extended northward into Syria and eastward across the Jordan. The Hittite Empire was more loosely organized. In the kingdom of Hatti proper, the king ruled through a council of leading men, probably great lords who owed him military service, primarily in chariots. The Hittite empire in Anatolia and Syria was a collection of tributary allies whose princes were bound to the Great King by intermarriage and other personal ties; beyond these was a fluctuating frontier zone where Hittite and Egyptian influence competed. How Mitanni was governed is unclear because its archives have never come to light – indeed its capital, Washukkani, has not even been located – but it seems likely that it resembled the

Gold plate from Ugarit, a rich city state on the Syrian coast, showing a hunting scene: an archer in a chariot pursues aurochs (wild cattle) and wild goat. Chariots were always favoured for hunting by Middle Eastern élites and this was probably their original function.

THE DEFENCES OF EGYPT
c. 1500 BC

The Middle Kingdom built the series of Nile forts down to Buhen. The New Kingdom extended the line south to Napata, near the Fourth Cataract, making the Nubian kingdom of Kush a province and Egyptianizing its population. Avaris in the delta was the capital of the Hyksos dynasty. It was taken and sacked in c. 1550 BC by Ahmose, who made Thebes the capital.

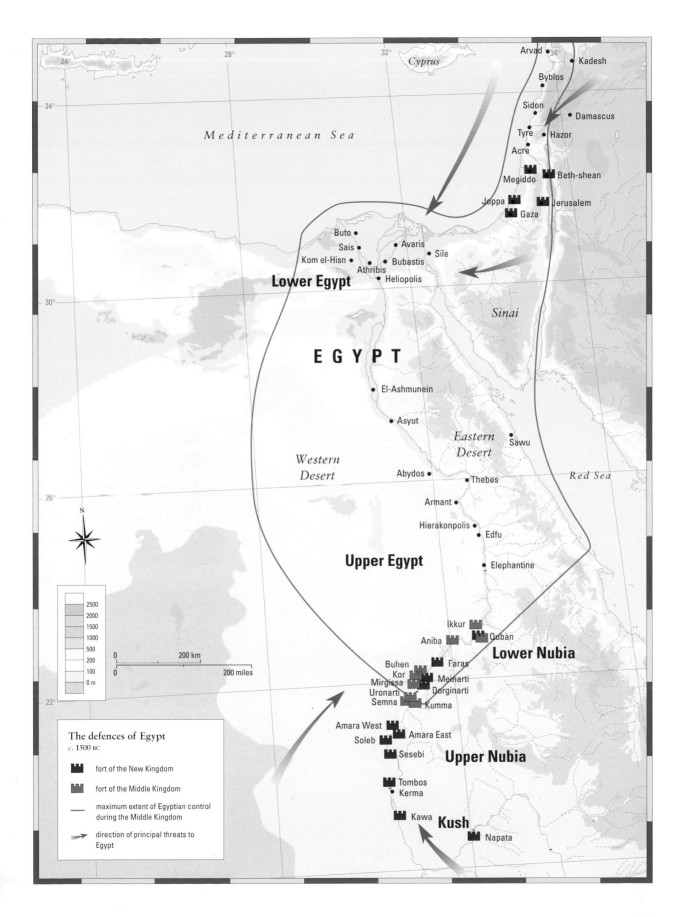

Arvad
Kadesh
Byblos
Sidon
Damascus
Tyre
Hazor
Acre
Megiddo
Beth-shean
Joppa
Jerusalem
Gaza

Mediterranean Sea

Cyprus

Buto
Sais
Avaris
Sile
Kom el-Hisn
Bubastis
Athribis
Heliopolis

Lower Egypt

Sinai

EGYPT

El-Ashmunein

Asyut

Eastern Desert
Sawu

Western Desert
Abydos
Thebes
Red Sea

Armant

Hierakonpolis
Edfu

Upper Egypt
Elephantine

Ikkur
Aniba
Quban

Lower Nubia

Buhen
Faras
Kor
Meinarti
Mirgissa
Dorginarti
Uronarti
Semna
Kumma

Amara West
Amara East
Soleb
Sesebi

Upper Nubia

Tombos
Kerma

Kawa
Kush
Napata

2500
2000
1500
1000
500
200
100
0 m

200 km
200 miles

The defences of Egypt
c. 1500 BC

fort of the New Kingdom

fort of the Middle Kingdom

maximum extent of Egyptian control during the Middle Kingdom

direction of principal threats to Egypt

Hittite more than the Egyptian model. Assyria, 'land of Assur', originally a small area around the city of Assur on the upper Tigris, had expanded by planting colonies over northern Mesopotamia and Assyrianizing the Hurrian population. The result was a kingdom smaller but more compact than either the Hittite or the Mitannian, and, as it turned out, with a greater future. Little is known about Kassite Babylonia.

Much is known about diplomacy, however, especially from the archives of fourteenth-century Egypt. The most striking feature is the militarization of society. In earlier times kings had been essentially religious leaders; in the High Bronze Age they are war leaders. The pharaohs of the Old and Middle Kingdom were portrayed as benign gods in calm repose; those of the New Kingdom are chariot warriors surrounded by their charioteers. When kings wrote to kings they

On a painted stele Ramesses II holds up three prisoners – an Asian, a Nubian, and a Libyan, representing the enemies of Egypt – by their hair before executing them. This stylized image, the king killing prostrate foreigners, is constantly repeated in Egyptian art.

commonly used a formal salutation, greeting first 'my brother the king' and then his wives, his chariots, his horses and his chief men – in that order. Kings saw themselves as constantly at war, surrounded by enemies, defending their gods against foreign gods. In the thirteenth century Tukuli-Ninurta I of Assyria addressed the following prayer to his god Assur:

> The foreign countries surround the city Ashur [Assur] from everywhere with a circle of evil, and their assemblage hates the shepherd you appointed to keep your people in order. All the lands that I gratified with a beneficial help despise you, and while you sheltered them with your protection, they repulse your country. The king you granted benefits is steadfast in his not agreeing, and those upon whom you established your favour prepare the weapons. For your city Ashur the work of the battlefield is standingly prepared, and all the onslaughts of the flood are raised against it. Your adversaries and enemies keep looking at the site of your residence, and they made a wicked agreement to plunder your country, Assyria. Night and day the foreign countries are longing for the destruction of your marvels, and apply themselves to destroy your towns from above and below.

War was an ordeal by battle to decide which king and which god were in the right. The Hittites actually conducted formal lawsuits against the enemy king and his gods to convict them of crimes before Hittite armies crossed the frontier. The Hittite king Mursilis sent this challenge to Uhha-ziti, king of Arzawa in western Anatolia:

> I came here, but I stopped before the border of your land. I did not invade your land, I did not take away prisoners, cattle and sheep. But you did begin the strife against my Sun, you did come, invade the land of Dankuwa and depopulate it. The gods will go at my side and decide the trial in my favour.

And so they did, according to the Hittite annals:

> When I began my march and arrived to Mt Lawasha, the Storm God my lord manifested his divine justice and sent a thunderbolt. My army saw the thunderbolt, and the Arzawa land saw it: and the thunderbolt … caused Uhha-ziti to fall to his knees and become sick.

When Tukuli-Ninurta of Assyria, whom we have already met, sacked Babylon, he despoiled its temples and carried off the statues of its gods. An Assyrian epic poem celebrating his deeds explains that this act was not really sacrilege, for the gods of Babylon had already deserted the Kassite king

Kashtiliash for the crime of oath-breaking, and Tukuli-Ninurta had merely ratified their decision:

> The gods were angry at the treacheries of the king of the Kassites, committed by the standard of Shamash. Against the oath-breaker Kashtiliash the gods of heaven and earth decided to send punishment: … Marduk abandoned his august sanctuary, the city of Babylon … Sin left Ur, his cult centre … With Sippar and Larsa Shamash became wroth … Ea abandoned Eridu, the house of wisdom … Ishtaran became angry with Der … Annunitu no longer approached Akkad … The Mistress of Uruk gave up her city …

A war had to have a just cause to receive the help of the gods. In addition, once begun the war had to be fought by the universally recognized rules, lest divine favour be lost. A formal challenge was expected. This convention went back to the Middle Bronze Age (compare the letter of Yarim-Lim quoted in the preceding chapter), but now kings are expected to offer pitched battle outside the city walls. Hittite kings wrote to their enemies: 'I came out against you: come out! If you do not come, I will subdue you like a bear, and you will die suffocated.' The challenger was expected to name the battlefield; Egyptian inscriptions complain that the Levantine nomads do not communicate the place or day of battle. Once on the battlefield a king was expected to charge the enemy directly, and ruses and surprises were considered cowardly.

THE BATTLE OF MEGIDDO

Educated people in the Western world always knew, from the testimony of the Homeric poems and the Bible, that chariots had played a major role in warfare before 1000 BC, but how they were used was a mystery. Only in recent years has chariot warfare received serious study, and the subject is still riddled with controversy. In the *Iliad*, composed at a time when chariots were no longer used in Greek wars, chariots do very little except transport leading warriors to the battlefield, where they immediately dismount and fight on foot. Some distinguished scholars have thought that the Homeric tradition is essentially accurate in its depiction of Bronze Age chariot warfare, and that chariots were nothing but prestige vehicles for men of rank. But that seems highly improbable. Chariots were simply too expensive. In addition to the acquisition of valuable horses and equipment, and the training of drivers and grooms, it has been estimated that 10 acres of prime grain land would have been required to feed one team of chariot horses, and we know that in the High Bronze Age any important prince maintained hundreds or thousands of such teams. It is difficult to see why they should have invested such resources in fleets of luxurious taxis that served no military function.

On the other hand, those who think chariots were actually used in battle have generally operated on the explicit or implicit assumption that their use must have been analogous to the function that cavalry has had in warfare since the early Iron Age, that is, ancillary to infantry. They imagine the chariots providing a screen for their own infantry before the battle; during the battle (which they presume was essentially an infantry engagement), seeking opportunities to deliver a decisive charge into any gap that might appear in the flank or rear of the enemy infantry; and pursuing the defeated infantry after the battle. These scenarios rest of course on the supposition, which most scholars of the period have never questioned, that disciplined infantry formations existed in the Bronze Age. But in the preceding chapter it is argued that in fact there were no reliable infantry formations capable of taking an offensive role in battle during the Early and Middle Bronze Age, and here it is argued that there were none in the High Bronze Age either. This means that any interpretation of chariot warfare of that period which assigns to it a role like that of cavalry in later warfare must be seriously mistaken; that infantry normally supported chariotry, not the other way around; and that High Bronze Age warfare must have been very different from any later warfare. Many will find this conclusion far too radical. The main reason for advancing it is because the widely held view that something similar to 'infantry', as we now understand it, was available in the High Bronze Age is an assumption that cannot easily be reconciled with our not inconsiderable information about the actual battles of this period. This we owe to Egyptian art, which had always focused on the

Thutmose III (reigned 1479– 1425 BC) fought seventeen campaigns in Asia. The first led to his great victory at Megiddo. The longest was the campaign of 1446 BC, when he crossed Syria and invaded the western part of the Mitannian kingdom.

glorification of the pharaoh, and under the New Kingdom naturally turned to the celebration of the pharaoh's military victories. We are left with sufficient epigraphic and pictorial records of two battles in the Levant – Megiddo in 1457 BC and Kadesh in 1275 BC – that we can, for the first time in history, attempt to reconstruct what happened on a battlefield.

Thutmose III, often called the greatest ruler of the Eighteenth Dynasty, came to the throne of Egypt as a boy, but for the first twenty years of his reign he was under the shadow of his stepmother, aunt and co-pharaoh, Hatshepsut. She called herself 'King' and 'His Majesty' and wore a false beard in portrait sculpture, but despite these masculine pretensions she showed little interest in military affairs and allowed the Egyptian position in the northern territories to deteriorate. Her death about 1460 was followed by a general revolt of the Canaanite allies. (The Egyptian word 'Canaan' usually designated Palestine, but sometimes it meant the entire Levant). Thutmose, who later smashed Hatshepsut's statues, immediately reversed her foreign policy. He led his army into Canaan to meet a coalition of princes said to number 330, led by the king of Kadesh. The rebels were based at the city of Megiddo, a strategic point which was the site of many battles in antiquity as it commanded the exit from the Pass of Aruna leading to the coastal plain of Palestine. The king of Kadesh sent Thutmose his challenge: 'I shall wait here in Megiddo.'

The young pharaoh marched from the Delta up the coastal plain in two weeks, at a rate of 15 miles a day, which in antiquity was the maximum for a large army. All the Great Kingdoms had sufficient bureaucratic resources to manage campaigns like this; otherwise they would not have been Great Kingdoms.

The Battle of Megiddo
1457 BC

Phase 1

1 Thutmose, marching north through the Pass of Aruna, camps by the brook and the next day deploys his chariot formations along the low hills around the plain of Megiddo, leaving his infantry to guard his camp

2 Meanwhile the King of Kadesh moves his army from the city placing his forces along the edge of the plateau

Megiddo

Plain of Megiddo

Pass of Aruna

Qina Brook

Armies still carried their own provisions, on ox wagon and pack donkey, but now they depended mostly on local governors and allied rulers for supplies, and all those along Thutmose's line of march will have been notified of his coming far in advance.

A day's march south of Megiddo he called a staff meeting to decide on the best route. According to the inscription later put up on the walls of the temple of Amun at Karnak, the officers advised they avoid the direct route, which led through the narrow Aruna Pass:

What is it like to go on this road which becomes so narrow? It is reported that the foe is there, waiting on the outside, while they are becoming more numerous. Will not horse have to go after horse, and the army and the people similarly? Will the vanguard of us be fighting while the rear guard is waiting here in Aruna unable to fight? Now two other roads are here. One of the roads – behold it is to the east of us, so that it comes out

THE BATTLE OF MEGIDDO 1457 BC

When this world ends the last battle will be fought at Megiddo (Armageddon in Greek), according to the New Testament prophecy (Revelation 16:16). Megiddo was also the site of the first battle that can be reconstructed in some detail. The reconstruction proposed here assumes infantry played no active role at all in the battle, which was purely a clash of chariots manoeuvring in squadrons.

Phase 2

3 Thutmose orders a general advance, his chariots forming into mobile squadrons

4 The King of Kadesh advances down the slope to engage the Egyptians, but things go badly wrong. The Egyptians rebuff his attack and drive the enemy from the battlefield. The King of Kadesh falls back within the city which is eventually taken

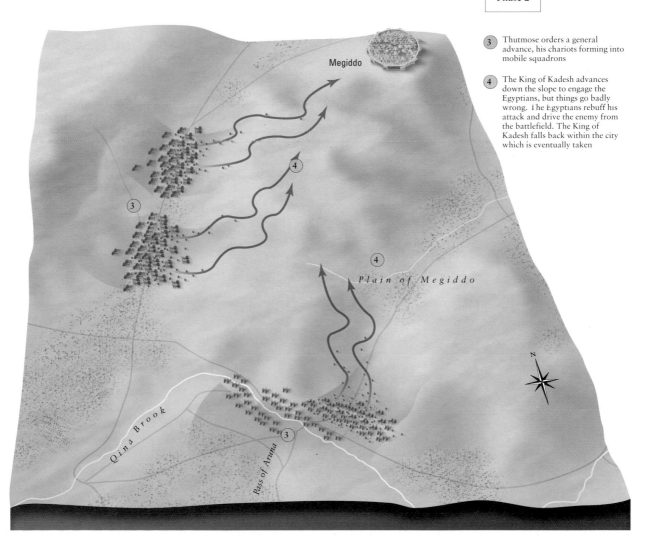

Under the Eighteenth Dynasty the gigantic temple complex at Karnak near Thebes became the centre of the imperial cult of Amun-Re and the starting point for the annual festival processions. On its walls Thutmose III inscribed a year-by-year account of his campaigns in the Levant.

at Taanach. The other – behold it is to the north side of Djefti, and we will come out to the north of Megiddo. Let our victorious lord proceed on the one of them which is satisfactory to his heart, but do not make us go on that difficult road.

But the pharaoh rejects this counsel:

'Behold,' they will say, these enemies whom Re abominates: 'Has his majesty set out upon another road because he has become afraid of us?' – so they will speak.

This report is not to be taken literally. Iconography demanded that a pharaoh be portrayed fighting almost single-handed against hordes of enemies, and his subordinates are included in the picture to serve as foils, their cowardice and folly setting off his wisdom and heroism. Later on, as the column nears the plain of

Megiddo, the humbled generals are allowed to save face by offering the pharaoh an obvious bit of tactical advice:

> Let our victorious lord listen to us this time, and let our lord guard for us the rear of his army and his people. When the rear of the army comes forth for us into the open, then we shall fight against these foreigners, then we shall not trouble our hearts about the rear of our army.

Of course Thutmose would not have attacked the Canaanites until his army was assembled. But even this elementary precaution he must seem to accede to solely out of concern for the rear of his army, not out of a healthy respect for his enemy. Once the army has debouched from the pass, a few miles from Megiddo and the Canaanite army, which makes no attempt to interfere, he decides to pitch camp and delay the battle until the morning.

Many commentators have assumed that the war council reported in the

Egyptian infantry on the march, from the tomb of Hatshepsut. The men are led in column by their officer. All are armed with spears, shields, and bronze-headed axes, and the soldier to the rear of the officer carries a bow case.

inscription must reflect tactical realities, and have wondered why the Canaanites passed up an obvious opportunity to attack the isolated Egyptian vanguard while the rest of their army was deploying onto the plain. This would indeed seem an obvious move to any modern army. But was it so obvious in the High Bronze Age? It is clear from this inscription, as well as from other campaigns where information exists, that armies met almost by appointment at a location known in advance, just as European armies did in the eighteenth century AD, and for the same reasons: military organization was highly sophisticated but transport was primitive, so that large armies required complicated logistical support and moved slowly along predetermined routes to carefully chosen battlefields. (Both kinds of army needed level and open ground, though for different technical reasons.) Fortifications provided an additional limiting factor in both periods, but were particularly decisive in the Bronze Age. No city walls were invulnerable to a besieger with sufficient resources, but sieges were long and costly, so time was on the side of the defender, especially when the besieger was as far from home as Thutmose was. Hence a defending army always sought to take up a position in front of a fortified city into which it could retreat in the event of defeat; and preferably as close as possible to the city walls, for in the event of a rout the enemy might get inside them before the gates closed, as nearly happened at Megiddo. The Canaanites had long since picked the battlefield by choosing Megiddo as their base, and their army was in an excellent defensive position, with the walls of Megiddo behind it and in front of it a brook called Qina, which may have presented a small natural obstacle. If the Canaanites had tried to attack Thutmose's vanguard they would have had to abandon this position. Hence the pharaoh may have felt little trepidation about rejecting his generals' over-cautious advice, if in fact they gave any.

But this is not to say that surprise was impossible. Strategic surprise may have been impractical, for the reasons given above, but there must have been considerable room for tactical surprise, or much more than there was in neoclassical European warfare, because of the speed with which chariotry could deploy on the battlefield. Both at Megiddo and at Kadesh the Egyptian inscriptions place much importance on the danger of being attacked before one's forces are fully prepared for battle, and at Kadesh a surprise attack really occurred.

To return to Megiddo: on the next morning Thutmose divided his forces into three groups and positioned them before the city, his left wing to the north-west of the city and his right on the south bank of the brook, with the pharaoh himself standing in a gold chariot at the centre of the line.

> Thereupon his majesty prevailed over them at the head of his army. Then they saw his majesty prevailing over them, and they fled headlong to Megiddo with faces of fear. They abandoned their horses and their chariots of gold and silver … Now the people had shut this town against them, but they let down garments to hoist them up into this town.

We are told the city might have been taken at this point had the Egyptians not been diverted from pursuit by the temptations of booty, especially the horses and chariots. Thutmose ordered the city to be taken by siege at all costs, 'inasmuch as every prince of every northern country is shut up in it, for the capturing of Megiddo is the capturing of a thousand towns'. Megiddo surrendered after a seven-month siege. As seven was a lucky number, historical events in the ancient Middle East had a tendency to fall on the seventh day or month or year, but we may safely take this to mean that the siege was a long one. The booty included

924 chariots, two of them gold; 2,041 horses; 502 bows; 340 living prisoners and 83 hands (Egyptians cut off the right hand or penis of a slain enemy as a trophy).

As always, we are given no details about the fighting itself. Pharaohs cannot really fight, they can only triumph. But some things can be inferred. There were at least a thousand chariots on the Canaanite side, and presumably the Egyptians brought a like number. We know from the archives of Ugarit in Syria and Cnossus in Crete that those important city states had a thousand chariots each, and from other sources that Great Kingdoms like Egypt and Hatti each kept several thousand chariots in their total forces. But to us the most surprising factor is the role of the infantry; or rather, its absence. The Egyptian infantry are mentioned on the march to Megiddo, but what were they doing in the battle? We only hear of chariots there, and we wonder how foot soldiers could have kept up with them. And where were the Canaanite foot soldiers? Only 83 Canaanites were killed and 340 taken prisoner, and this in a general rout that included 2,000 charioteers, many of whom must have been killed or captured. I suggest that in fact the infantry did not participate in the fighting at all, nor were they expected to do so. The Canaanite infantry were guarding the city walls, and the Egyptian infantry were guarding the Egyptian camp. But before we examine the implications of this hypothesis let us consider the larger and better-known battle at Kadesh.

Life-size black granite statue of Ramesses II (reigned 1279–1212 BC), best-known pharaoh of the Nineteenth Dynasty. As soon as he assumed the blue crown he challenged the Hittites for the mastery of Syria. In 1276 BC he led his armies north to Byblos. The next year came the great battle at Kadesh.

THE BATTLE OF KADESH

The great victory at Megiddo was only the first of seventeen campaigns that Thutmose III waged in Canaan, eventually extending the Egyptian frontier to the Euphrates. But under his successors Syria was lost to the Hittites and the energies of the Eighteenth Dynasty were dissipated in the bizarre religious reformation of the pharaoh Akhenaten and the counter-reformation that followed. At the end of the fourteenth century the Nineteenth Dynasty took over, determined to restore the traditional gods and boundaries of Egypt. When the Syrian principality of Amurru switched its allegiance from Egypt to Hatti this provoked a confrontation between Mutawallis II, the Hittite king, and Ramesses II of Egypt. The ensuing engagement at Kadesh may have been the biggest battle of the High Bronze Age, hence in all history to that date. It is certainly the best-documented battle before classical Greece, because Ramesses later bestowed upon it unprecedented commemoration through an elaborate pictorial history and narrative inscribed on the walls of many Egyptian temples.

In the spring of 1275 BC Mutawallis 'collected together all the foreign countries as far as the end of the sea' (so said the Egyptians, characteristically disinclined to underestimate the numbers of their foes), and moved down to Kadesh in Syria, a strongly fortified city at the southern edge of the Hittite Empire. Ramesses made the march from Egypt to Syria in only one month, bringing four divisions of the Egyptian army, named Amun, Re, Ptah and Seth after their patron gods. The division of Amun, under the pharaoh himself, was in the lead, with the other three strung out behind. Some 8 miles to the south of Kadesh Ramesses camped on the banks of the Orontes, where he received misleading information from two nomads, who told him the Hittite army was still far in the north. The Egyptian records present these two bedouin as Hittite spies who had been instructed 'to prevent His Majesty's army from making ready to fight'. (But how did the Egyptians know that?) Ramesses crossed the Orontes with the

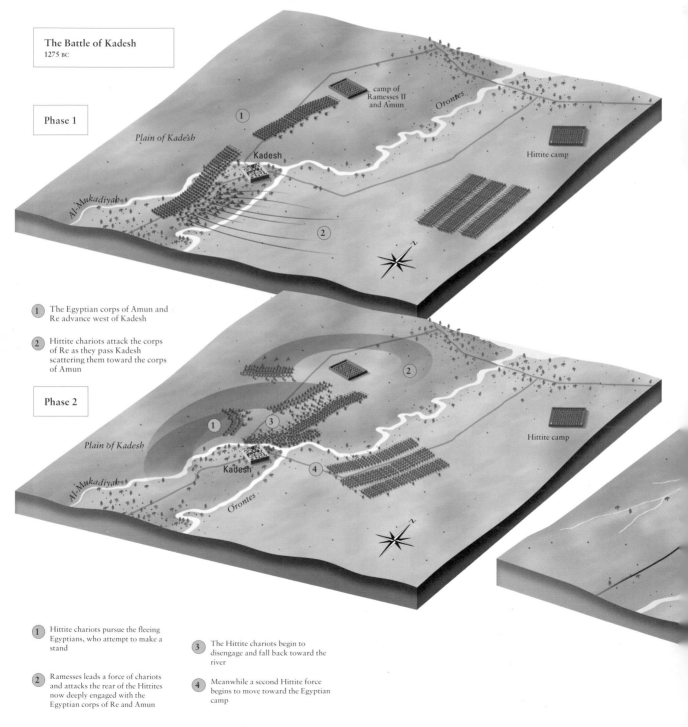

The Battle of Kadesh
1275 BC

Phase 1

Plain of Kadesh

camp of Ramesses II and Amun

Orontes

Kadesh

Al-Mukadiyah

Hittite camp

① The Egyptian corps of Amun and Re advance west of Kadesh

② Hittite chariots attack the corps of Re as they pass Kadesh scattering them toward the corps of Amun

Phase 2

Plain of Kadesh

Al-Mukadiyah

Kadesh

Orontes

Hittite camp

① Hittite chariots pursue the fleeing Egyptians, who attempt to make a stand

② Ramesses leads a force of chariots and attacks the rear of the Hittites now deeply engaged with the Egyptian corps of Re and Amun

③ The Hittite chariots begin to disengage and fall back toward the river

④ Meanwhile a second Hittite force begins to move toward the Egyptian camp

division of Amun, marched north across the plain of Kadesh, and pitched camp north-west of the city. Then his scouts captured two Hittite scouts, who were tortured until they revealed that the Hittite camp lay only a few miles to the east: 'They are furnished with their infantry and their chariotry carrying their weapons of warfare, and they are more numerous than the sand of the river-banks. See, they stand equipped and ready to fight behind Kadesh the Old.' Ramesses called a staff meeting, rebuked his officers for their poor intelligence work, and sent his vizier to bring up quickly the rest of the army. The division of Re, which was still in the previous night's camp, crossed the Orontes and moved north, presumably at the double, towards the camp of the pharaoh.

But the wretched Chief of Khatti [Hatti] stood in the midst of the army which was with him and did not come out to fight through fear of His Majesty. But he had sent men and horses exceeding many and multitudinous like the sand, and they were three men on a chariot and they were equipped with all weapons of warfare. They had been made to

THE BATTLE OF KADESH 1275 BC

Much about the battle of Kadesh is open to conjecture, such as the 'coming of the Ne'arin of Pharoah from the land of Amor'. 'Ne'arin' is a Semitic word meaning 'young men' and it has been suggested these were Syrian auxiliaries, perhaps chariot-runners. As they are the only soldiers other than Ramesses given any credit on the reliefs they probably made a significant contribution.

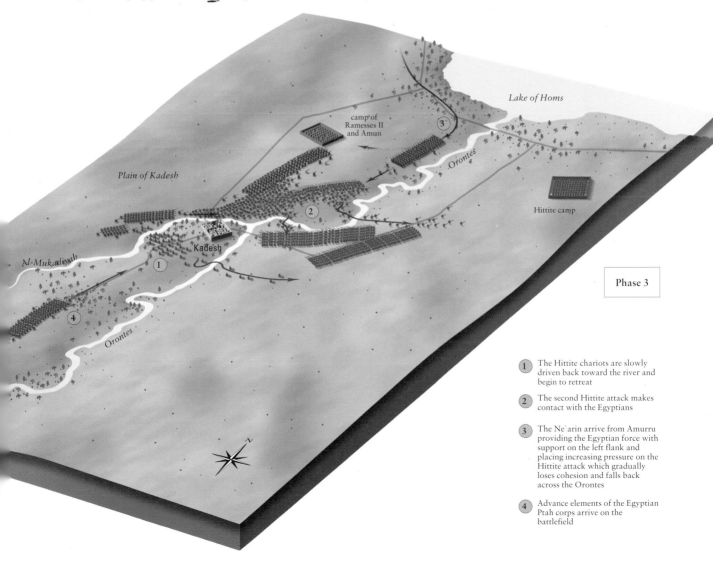

Plain of Kadesh

camp of Ramesses II and Amun

Lake of Homs

Orontes

Hittite camp

Al-Mukadiyah

Kadesh

Orontes

N

Phase 3

① The Hittite chariots are slowly driven back toward the river and begin to retreat

② The second Hittite attack makes contact with the Egyptians

③ The Ne'arin arrive from Amurru providing the Egyptian force with support on the left flank and placing increasing pressure on the Hittite attack which gradually loses cohesion and falls back across the Orontes

④ Advance elements of the Egyptian Ptah corps arrive on the battlefield

OPPOSITE: *On the left, two-man Egyptian chariots. On the right, three-man Hittite chariots. 'His Majesty was after them like a griffin ... I lifted up my voice to call to my army, saying: "Stand ye firm, steady your hearts, my army, that you may behold my victory, I being alone..."' On the reliefs, however, he does not appear quite alone.*

Detail from the Kadesh reliefs. The legend reads: 'The coming of Pharoah's scout bringing two scouts of the Fallen one of Khatti into the Pharoah's Presence. They beat them to make them say where the wretched Fallen one of Khatti was.' On the upper register the royal chariot is made ready.

stand concealed behind the town of Kadesh, and now they came forth from the south side of Kadesh and broke into the army of Pre' [Re] in its midst as they were marching and did not know nor were they prepared to fight. Thereupon the infantry and the chariotry of His Majesty were discomfited before them...

After routing the army of Re, the Hittite force turned northward and attacked the camp, which the division of Amun was still setting up. In the reliefs we see that many of the Egyptian chariot horses had been unyoked. 'Then the host of the Khatti enemy hemmed in the followers of His Majesty ...' The reliefs show that at some point Hittites got inside the camp itself. Ramesses put on his armour, mounted his chariot, and attacked the Hittites on the western side of the camp.

Then His Majesty started forth at a gallop, and entered into the host of the fallen ones of Khatti, being alone by himself and none other with him. So then His Majesty went to look about him and he found 2,500 chariots hemming him in on his outer side, consisting of all the champions of the fallen ones of Khatti with the many foreign countries which were with them... [trans. Gardiner; but Drews has suggested 'consisting of all the champions' should be rendered 'together with all the

runners'. These 'runners', whose role will be discussed later, were light infantrymen who ran beside the chariots in battle.]

At this crisis Ramesses had a long conversation with Amun, reminding the god of all he had done for him and receiving Amun's warm encouragement; this he needed, as he was fighting alone, assisted, we are told repeatedly, only by his driver Menna and his two horses Mut-Is-Contented and Victory-in-Thebes (though the narrative at one point admits that he was in fact accompanied by men of his household, and the reliefs show other Egyptian chariots in action).

I shot on my right and captured with my left. I was in their sight like Sutekh at his moment. I found the 2,500 chariots, in whose midst I was, sprawling before my horse ... all their arms were weak, and they were unable to shoot.

Mutawallis, still afraid to enter the fighting himself (or such is the ungenerous assessment of his motives in the Egyptian sources), now sent

Ramesses kills a Hittite and tramples on another. 'The goodly god, powerful of strength, great of victories, defeating all foreign countries, King who slays his enemies with his single arm ... he entered in among the Khatti enemies, being like a storm which goes forth from heaven and his might like fire in stubble ...'

reinforcements across the Orontes, consisting of an additional 1,000 chariots led by the king's own brothers and allied chiefs. Ramesses fought on 'alone' but found time to berate his absent men at length for their cowardly desertion and their ingratitude for his past benefactions. His driver, Menna, implored him to leave the battle, but the king replied:

> 'Stand firm, steady thy heart, my shield-bearer. I will enter in among them like the pounce of a falcon, killing, slaughtering and casting to the ground. What careth thy heart for these effeminate ones at millions of whom I take no pleasure?' [Apparently Ramesses is referring to his own followers.] Thereupon His Majesty started forth quickly and entered at a gallop into the midst of the battle for the sixth time of entering in amongst them. I was after them like Ba'al at the moment of his power ... ['I' is Ramesses. The narration shifts abruptly between the third and first person.]

The outcome may have been affected by the arrival of the third Egyptian army, the division of Ptah, from the south, but the official record, in its single-minded concentration on pharaonic heroics, has no time for such things. (The reliefs do, however, depict the timely arrival of certain Egyptian reinforcements, apparently Syrian auxiliaries, who killed the Hittites who were plundering the camp.) In any case the Hittites were eventually driven across the Orontes, into which they dived 'even as crocodiles plunge', and took refuge inside Kadesh.

The next day fighting was resumed. This was probably a more conventional kind of battle, but it must have been inconclusive, as the literary record describes it in the vaguest terms and the pictorial record not at all. Evidently the Egyptians did not succeed in driving the Hittites inside Kadesh and so could not lay siege to the city. The two kings agreed to a truce, which the Egyptian record naturally portrays as an act of submission by the Hittite, and Ramesses took his army back to Egypt. Fifteen years later Egypt and Hatti signed a peace treaty recognizing one another's spheres of influence, and Ramesses married a Hittite princess.

The task of disentangling historical fact from literary and artistic convention is more complicated here than in the Megiddo inscription. In the first place, it is very difficult to believe that the Egyptians were really ignorant of the location of the Hittite camp, which was only a few miles from their own. Everyone had known for weeks that the battle was to be at Kadesh. It is clear from the Egyptian record that armies, as we would expect, made every effort to get information about the movements of the enemy, bringing in passing nomads for questioning, and sending out scouts on chariot or horseback. It was conventional to attribute cowardly and dishonourable ruses to the enemy, but there is so much emphasis on the Hittite 'ruse' at Kadesh that one suspects an attempt to cover up some serious blunder on the part of the Egyptians. Once we look for it, the nature of the blunder seems evident. Ramesses had picked the worst possible site for his camp.

OVERLEAF: *Hittites retreat to Kadesh. 'I caused them to plunge into the water even as crocodiles plunge, fallen upon their faces one upon the other. I killed among them according as I willed. Not one of them looked behind him, nor was there any other who turned round. Whoever among them fell, he did not raise himself.'*

An army was in a vulnerable position at the moment of its arrival at the designated battlefield, as it would take considerable time to deploy from marching column into battle line, and there was always a risk of being attacked before the line was fully formed. At Megiddo, where this risk was unusually acute owing to the narrowness of the approach, the Egyptian vanguard, as soon as it reached the plain, had stood guard until the rest of the army emerged from the defile. But at Kadesh the pharaoh, instead of waiting for the division of Re to come up, advanced so far that he finally pitched his camp north of the city, a position which required the rest of his army to cross the entire plain of Kadesh in the sight of the Hittites, who could observe all significant troop movements on the plain from the walls of the city on its high mound. As in eighteenth-century AD Europe, ruses were bad form; but that was because they were usually bad tactics too, and no one could be blamed for seizing an opportunity like this. So Mutawallis is likely to have reasoned when he sent 2,500 chariots – the bulk of his chariotry, probably including all the Hittite chariots but not their allies – to cross the Orontes at a ford south of the city, screened by the wooded banks of the river. (It is possible the Egyptians were ignorant of the existence of this ford, and this might explain their false sense of security.) The Hittite chariots hit the division of Re as it marched in column, probably demolishing it as an organized unit, as there is no further mention of it in the battle. The Hittites then swung northward and attacked the camp of Amun; they were soon reinforced by the rest of their chariotry, which crossed the river by a ford north of the city. Ramesses held them off with such chariot squadrons as he could muster.

The attempt to reconstruct exactly what was going on requires some exercise of the imagination, for it was certainly unlike any kind of battle known to later history. The main difference was that chariots, if the interpretation advanced here is correct, were purely and simply missile platforms. (Often it is said that Hittite chariots were armed with long spears instead of bows, because that is how they are usually portrayed on the Kadesh reliefs. But to use a thrusting spear from a fast-moving chariot would be a physical impossibility. Probably the Hittite charioteers were deprived of their bows on these reliefs only by Egyptian iconographic convention. Even the Egyptian poem betrays the fact that the Hittites at Kadesh carried bows – they were 'unable to shoot', 'unable to take up a bow' – and there is plenty of other evidence that Hittite charioteers, like all other charioteers of the period, were archers. All chariots carried in addition a long spear, but as a last-ditch weapon.) As missile platforms, chariots would have been useful only in a linear formation, like warships in the age of sail, and like sailing ships they would have been most effective firing broadside to the enemy; but they were also capable of much more flexible tactics than warships. Various sources suggest that chariots were commonly organized into squadrons of fifty, each under a captain. These could have operated as independent tactical units, but in battles on the scale of Megiddo and Kadesh the squadrons must have been formed into larger groups. They could have opened their charge in a linear formation, drawn up in one, two, or perhaps three lines. The thousand Egyptian chariots at Megiddo, if drawn up in a single line, would have stretched for two miles. Or they might have been organized into columns or wedge formations. The 2,500 Hittite chariots that crossed the Orontes ford were obviously not in a linear formation. However they formed, the charioteers would have begun firing as soon as they came within extreme bowshot of the enemy, or about 200 yards, for they are portrayed in art as shooting over the heads of their own horses. On the other hand, how else could artists portray them? It is difficult to believe they normally charged straight into the enemy line, a move which would surely have meant prohibitive casualties. At Kadesh, Ramesses is supposed to have charged six times into the Hittites, which is hardly credible if we suppose these charges were carried all the way home. It seems more likely that when they came within effective bowshot, perhaps a hundred yards, the chariots in some fashion deployed into a linear formation, turned and galloped past or around the enemy line; or possibly divided into two lines, one turning right and the other left. If the enemy line were still intact, they could have wheeled away, regrouped and charged again.

The Hittites are said to have had 3,500 chariots at Kadesh, apparently 2,500 Hittite and 1,000 allied, and as a Hittite chariot normally carried three men – archer, driver and shield-bearer – instead of the standard two, there will have been more than 10,000 men in their chariot forces. Their infantry are said to have numbered 17,000 (or perhaps 37,000 – the reading is difficult). But the Hittite infantry are not mentioned at all in the battle. In the Egyptian reliefs they guard the gates of the city, and that seems to have been their only function. We are not told the size of the Egyptian forces but we suppose they were comparable. Egyptian divisions sometimes numbered 5,000, which would give us a figure of 20,000 for Ramesses' whole army. It is clear that each of the four Egyptian divisions contained both chariotry and infantry. The Egyptian infantry are mentioned on the march, but not in the battle. Apparently they were left to guard the camp, which on the reliefs is surrounded by a row of great oblong infantry shields. The shields form a cordon, offering sufficient protection against enemy arrows so that a chariot with a wounded crewman might retire behind it. It seems probable that in wars between civilized kingdoms heavy infantry was normally used only in these defensive roles, guarding camps and city walls, and for siege work. It would hardly have been possible for them to keep up with chariots in the field. Infantry will have operated independently only against barbarian tribes in hill country, where chariots could not go. Operations of this kind would not have required tight infantry formations, and there is no evidence any such existed.

There seem to have been two types of heavy infantryman, one armed with long spear and big shield, the other with a bow – a self bow, not the deadly composite bow. We may suppose these were conscripts, not trained professionals like the chariot crews. There is no evidence of mass conscription, but there were various forms of selective military draft. In Egypt every temple was obliged, when called upon, to send to the pharaoh's army one man in ten from its dependants. Such units are unlikely to have been highly trained or motivated.

But there is also evidence of a light infantry described as 'runners', usually armed with small shields and javelins, who followed the chariots to pick off those of the enemy that were disabled and to rescue the crews of those disabled on their own side. They are sometimes depicted in art as running beside the chariots. Perhaps they rode on them before arriving at the battlefield. On the Kadesh reliefs these skirmishers are seen killing or cutting off the hands of Hittite charioteers who have fallen from their vehicles. Peasant conscripts would not have been tough enough for this work; most chariot-runners were doubtless professional mercenaries, recruited from the barbarous tribes of the hinterlands. The Kadesh poem declares that the Hittite king 'left no silver in his land' when he came to Kadesh because of the great numbers of mercenaries he had to hire. Sometimes a small squad of runners seems to have been attached to every chariot. Often these light infantry were called *Sherden* (Sardinians), for many were recruited from that island; they can be distinguished in art by their distinctive horned helmets. Many others came from the high country of Anatolia and the Levant, the Libyan Desert and distant Nubia.

THE FALL OF THE CHARIOT KINGDOMS

This spectacular civilization collapsed with astonishing suddenness. Within a few decades, around 1200 BC, practically all the cities and palaces of the eastern Mediterranean basin north of Egypt were sacked and destroyed by enemies. The Mycenaean culture of the Aegean disappeared utterly, except for the hazy recollections of a lost world that turn up in Greek mythology and the Homeric poems. In western Asia the destruction was not so total; the art of writing survived, and city life eventually revived; but the Hittite kingdom was obliterated and nothing replaced it. The kingdom of Egypt survived after beating off many invasions, but lost its empire in the Levant and was never again to be a dominant power in the Middle East.

Egyptian inscriptions have left us the only contemporary records of this mysterious catastrophe. In 1208 BC the pharaoh Merneptah, son of Ramesses II, defeated an invading army of Libyans, who were accompanied by many northern allies, especially the people known to the Egyptians as *Ekwesh* (Achaeans), with other groups who can be identified as Sardinians, Sicilians, Tyrrhenians (Italians) and Luwians (Anatolians). Twenty years later the Nineteenth Dynasty faded away and was replaced by the Twentieth, which was to be the last of the great dynasties. In 1179 BC Ramesses III defeated invasions on both land and sea by Philistines from the coast of Canaan, accompanied by other barbarians. The inscription commemorating his victories says, 'The foreign countries made a conspiracy in their islands … No land could stand before their arms.' They defeated the Hittites and other countries in the north and then came against Egypt. 'They laid their hands upon the lands as far as the circuit of the earth …'

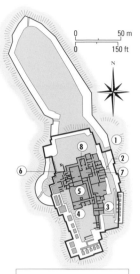

Tiryns citadel

— old citadel 1400 BC

① main gateway

② inner gateway to palace

③ greater propælum

④ lesser propælum

⑤ court to chief Megaron

⑥ chief Megaron

⑦ court to lesser Megaron

⑧ lesser Megaron

Hence the invaders are commonly called the 'Peoples of the Sea'; but the Egyptian language had no word for island, and the term 'isles' may be better translated as 'coastlands'. In their inscriptions kings had always portrayed themselves surrounded by hordes of enemies. Now rhetoric had become reality.

It was once thought that massive barbarian migrations must have been responsible for the disasters, but there is no evidence for any large population movements. It was believed that these invasions brought the Greeks or Achaeans (which is what the Greeks call themselves in the Homeric poems) into Greece. But when the Linear B script used in the Mycenaean world was finally deciphered in the 1950s it unexpectedly turned out to be a sort of Greek, which means that the Achaeans of Homer were already in Greece in the High Bronze Age. There was a tradition, recorded in the Bible (Amos 9:7, Jeremiah 47:4), that the Philistines had originally come from 'Caphtor' (Crete), so it was assumed they were part of the general *Völkerwanderung*. But the later Philistines, as revealed by archaeology, were as thoroughly Semitic and Canaanite as any people in Canaan, which would

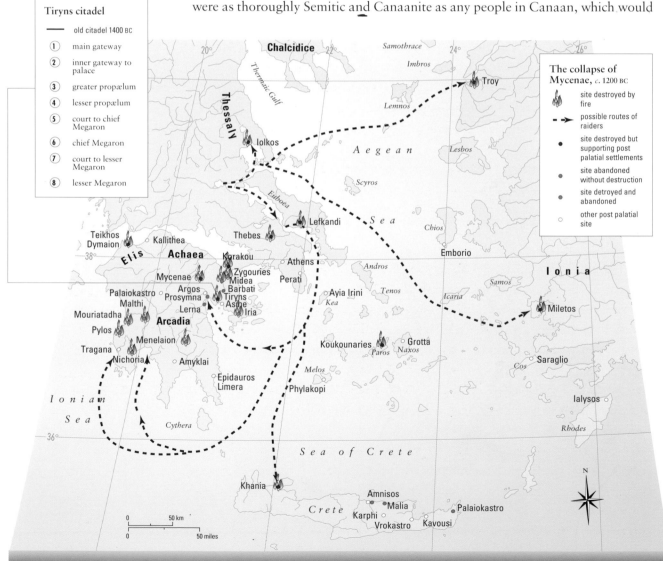

later be called Palestine after them; the legend of Cretan origins possibly started with a band of Achaean refugees who settled in Canaan during the upheavals around 1200 BC. The Indo-European invaders who inaugurated the chariot age have been compared to the medieval Normans; the invaders who ended it were more like Vikings, destructive raiders who founded no lasting dynasties and left nothing behind in the cities they ruined, many of which were never inhabited again. It was once thought that they brought iron weapons, but iron was still rare in the Middle East at this time and did not generally replace bronze as the common metal until after 1000 BC. The transition from Bronze Age to Iron Age could have been in some way a result of the fall of the palaces, but could not have caused it.

The end of the Early Bronze Age a thousand years before might be explained in terms of systems collapse. The High Bronze Age societies, however, do not seem to have been under any unusual stresses on the eve of their fall. There is no evidence for general environmental deterioration; and warfare was not becoming more frequent in the thirteenth century, rather the contrary. Pitched battles between Great Kings seem to have been rare in the High Bronze Age. Great Kings were expected to go on campaigns from time to time to show that they were Great Kings, especially at the start of a reign, but these martial demonstrations were largely symbolic. This is virtually admitted in a letter written by the old Hittite king Hattusilis III to a young Assyrian king who had just been enthroned:

> I have heard that my brother is grown into a man and goes often to hunt … My brother, you should not stay at home. Go out into the enemy country and defeat the enemy! But when you go out, go against a country on which you are three or four times superior.

A young king must prove his valour, but let him pick a small enemy. In addition to keeping up appearances, the raid will serve a useful purpose, as it will overawe his client states and perhaps acquire some new ones. Ramesses II was unusual in selecting another Great Kingdom for his target. But even Ramesses never fought another major campaign after Kadesh, even though he lived on for more than sixty years. The High Bronze Age states, it has been argued here, were the first to be capable of offensive warfare; but it would be wrong to think of warfare as endemic among them, in the sense that it was in classical Greek and Roman times.

Hence the most plausible explanation so far offered for this catastrophe is that it was a result of the transition from chariot to infantry warfare. The High Bronze Age states, because of their exclusive reliance on chariot armies, had always been vulnerable to concentrated infantry attack, but it was a long time before their vulnerability was perceived. Chariots, so deadly to heavy infantry, could easily be disabled by swarms of light infantry with missile weapons. Archaeology suggests that the weapon which accounted for most of the chariots

THE COLLAPSE OF MYCENAE, c. 1200 BC

All the main centres around the Aegean, including the mighty fortifications at Mycenae and Tiryns, were sacked and burned during the late thirteenth and early twelfth centuries, and Mycenaean civilization was obliterated. The same story was repeated all around the eastern Mediterranean. Dozens of palaces and cities were destroyed in Anatolia, Cyprus, Syria, and Palestine. The last documents from Ugarit suggest the city was attacked from the sea. Only in the interior of Palestine did some significant towns escape, such as Jerusalem.

This relief from Medinet Habu shows the sea battle Ramesses III won in his eighth year (1179 BC) over the Peleset (Philistines) and their allies, who attacked Egypt from the east. The invaders' ships, trapped in the mouth of the Nile, were raked by Egyptian archers. Another invading army was defeated in a land battle in Palestine.

was the simple javelin, most ancient and basic of missiles. This was a poor weapon compared to the composite bow, which was arguably the most effective firepower known before the nineteenth century AD. But composite bows were expensive machines that took years to make, and the training of an archer took years more. Javelins were cheap and abundant and any active young man could throw them. Active, poor and hungry young men were one commodity the barbarian world produced in unlimited numbers. Many such young men had learned about chariots in the service of the Great Kings, who had long recruited their chariot-runners from the tribes of the deserts and mountains and the islands of the sea.

At Medinet Habu Ramesses III smites his enemies in the traditional pose. His inscription claims that those who invaded Egypt in his eighth year were the same ones who had overthrown the Hittites and other kingdoms of the north, but it was conventional rhetoric to portray enemies as part of a vast coalition.

Some dramatic event must have revealed the vulnerability of the chariot armies. Perhaps it was the Achaean sack of Troy. The city known as Troy VI to archaeologists was destroyed in the late thirteenth century BC, and it is hard to explain the mesmerizing effect of the Trojan War on the later Greek imagination if something similar to that event had not happened. If so, the Achaeans who took Troy should be pictured as tribesmen from the Greek mountains, not the civilized Achaeans of Mycenae and Cnossus, though later legend mixed them up. Legend has it that the Trojans were 'tamers of horses', and that Achilles was killed by an arrow. This would have happened in the last years of Ramesses II (died 1212 BC), under whom the eastern Mediterranean world had enjoyed a long peace. After he died, the news from the north inspired a Berber chieftain to think the

unthinkable; that with this new method of fighting Egypt itself might be taken, and for this he recruited great numbers of javelin-men from all over the north. Then the sacking of cities began. It might well seem to the Egyptians that the foreigners had made a conspiracy on their coasts to seize the circuit of the earth.

Kingdoms that survived the collapse had to learn a new art of war. Egypt beat off the invasions by relying on infantry armies. Why Mesopotamia remained immune is not entirely clear, but the Assyrian kingdom served as a shield against invaders from the west, and it is possible that Assyria, a hilly land that had never been counted as one of the major chariot states, may have depended already upon a militia of foot soldiers. The early Iron Age was to be a world of such infantry militias, like the host of Israel in Canaan and the Dorian spearmen of Greece.

Ramesses III with his Philistine captives. They wear a distinctive headdress of feathers or hair. Later many became Egyptian mercenaries and were settled in garrisons in Palestine. The Sherden (Sardinians), with horned helmets, are shown fighting on both sides. (See endpapers.)

CHAPTER FIVE

THE WARS OF THE EMPIRES 1100–539 BC

IN 653 BC THE ASSYRIANS *inflicted a decisive defeat on the Elamites at the Ulai River in south-west Iran. On this relief from Ashurbanipal's palace at Nineveh, the Assyrian infantry drive back the Elamites. On the left an Assyrian holds up the head of the king of Elam. On the upper register vultures pick at dead Elamites. In the Iron Age infantry took the offensive and became the 'queen of battle'. Mass infantry armies gave rise to imperial states of unprecedented size and complexity.*

THE WARS OF THE EMPIRES

CHANGES IN WARFARE ON LAND AND SEA

The Iron Age dawned upon a world without great powers. Egypt, impoverished by the loss of her empire, lived on the memories of past glories. The feckless pharaohs of the Twenty-First Dynasty could not even keep out the nomads of the desert, and early in the tenth century they were replaced by a dynasty of Libyan origin. The Aegean basin and the Anatolian plateau were sunk in a dark age in which even the art of writing was lost. The Assyrian kingdom alone survived the catastrophe intact, and even enjoyed a spurt of expansion around 1100 BC under

Neo-Hittite slinger. After the fall of the Hittite kingdom c. 1200 BC a rump of Hittite culture survived at Carchemish, Aleppo, and other city states of north Syria and the Taurus. Many served as mercenaries, like the unfortunate Uriah the Hittite whose wife Bathsheba caught the eye of King David.

Tiglath-Pileser I, whose armies campaigned west into Anatolia and east into Iran; but his ephemeral empire died with him, for it proved unable to cope with the new challenge rising in the west.

In the Levant the withdrawal of the Egyptians and the obliteration of the Hittites left a power vacuum, in which the native peoples found themselves free of outside interference and for the first time in history took centre stage. The initial beneficiaries of the new situation were the Aramaeans. In the early eleventh century, when they first appear in Assyrian documents, the 'land of Aram' was located around the upper Euphrates, and the Aramaeans were one of many nomad groups roaming the edges of the Syrian Desert. Ever since agriculture began, shepherds like these had tended their flocks on the outskirts of arable

THE MIDDLE EAST c. 900 BC

A world without great powers. By this time Egypt has fallen into the Third Intermediate Period: the Libyan pharaohs at Tanis preside over a weakening state, eventually to be overshadowed by the Nubian kingdom of Kush. The Levant is divided among warring principalities (see next map).

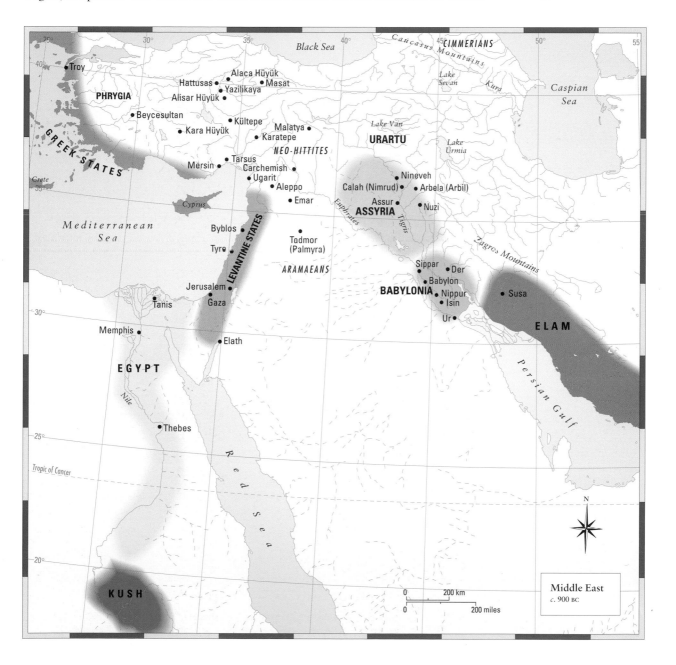

lands, but true nomad pastoralism capable of traversing the deep steppes and deserts had to await the domestication of horses and camels. Horse nomadism, which had conquered the European steppe back in the fourth millennium BC, never worked in the arid Middle East; but by the beginning of the Iron Age the Arabian camel had been domesticated, and the Aramaeans were the first to fully exploit its potential. From their strategic location at the bend of the Fertile Crescent they began in the eleventh century to move out in all directions, opening up a vast network of caravan routes, infiltrating the settled lands and settling there in increasing numbers as merchants, shepherds and farmers. Many other nomads, Amorites in the north and Arabs in the south, adopted the Aramaic language and culture, as did the Hittite cities of western Syria. Aramaic, a West Semitic dialect related to Amorite, was written in a convenient alphabetic script at least as early as the ninth century BC; it soon became the lingua franca of the Middle East, replacing Akkadian as the diplomatic language, and within a few centuries was to become the common tongue of all Mesopotamia and the Levant.

Most scholars have emphasized the commercial aspects of the Aramaean diaspora, but it had also a military side. Aramaeans often came as conquerors and rulers as well as traders. They founded many dynasties across Syria and Mesopotamia. As early as the eleventh century there arose in eastern Syria the aggressive kingdom of Zobah, which in the following century succeeded in pushing the Assyrians out of the Euphrates valley. These conquests went unrecorded, but a plausible guess can be made concerning the reasons for Aramaean military success. Warfare in the early Iron Age seems to have relied to an unprecedented extent on foot soldiers in the offensive. The major wars of the late twelfth and early eleventh centuries were those of Tiglath-Pileser, about which nothing is known, except that they were mostly fought in mountainous terrain, which suggests that they were infantry campaigns. Soon after that the formidable Assyrian kingdom became oddly helpless before the advancing Aramaean tribes. The Aramaeans therefore must have been highly effective infantry, and only one thing could give spearmen on foot a routine advantage over warriors who were similarly equipped. The Aramaeans, like the Dorian Greeks who overran the Peloponnesus around the same time, were probably pioneers in the art of fighting in formation. If so, we should not imagine Aramaeans fighting in a deep formation like the later Greek phalanx; more likely they could form only one or two ragged lines. But in the eleventh century that, combined with their alarming mobility, may have been enough. They could emerge unexpectedly from the desert on camelback, dismount and charge in a relatively disciplined line, presenting enough of a shield-wall to provide short-term protection from missiles. There was no longer any chariotry to deal with, and as yet no cavalry. Later the Assyrian Empire would recruit its best light infantry from the tribes of Aram.

The Aramaean example may have spurred a comparable military development, which took place a little later in the southern Levant, the land known to the Egyptians as Canaan and to the Romans as Palestine. After the collapse of Egypt the main players there were the Philistine towns on the coast and the semi-pastoral Hebraic tribes in the hills. At first the Philistines, who had a leading role in the catastrophe of about 1200 BC, seem to have replaced Egypt as the dominant power. According to the historical books of the Hebrew Bible (written down in their present form in the sixth century BC, but based on much older written and oral materials), in about 1050 BC the Philistines exacted tribute from the tribes of Israel and carried off the Ark of the Covenant, totem of their god Yahweh. But soon after, the Israelite federation set up a monarchy to lead it in war and turned the tables on the Philistines. In about 1000 David united the tribal federations of Israel and Judah with his capital at Jerusalem and created the strongest state in the region, levying tribute not only on the Philistines but upon the other Canaanite princes – Ammon, Moab, Edom – and even the Aramaean kingdom of Damascus in the north.

Despite the revisionist efforts of some recent biblical scholars, there is no serious reason to doubt the Hebrew traditions concerning the importance of the Davidic kingdom, which under David and his son Solomon was probably the most formidable state in the world. This was possible because competition was light in the tenth century,

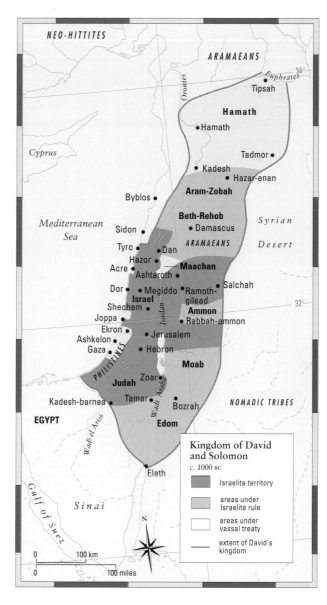

but also because the new art of war gave a great advantage to small cohesive states like Israel and the Aramaean principalities. The High Bronze Age had been a world of large monarchies and small élite armies; the early Iron Age was a world of small city states and tribal groups, and it is clear both from Hebrew tradition and archaeology that military success was a matter of disciplined mass infantry armed with spear and long iron sword. Hebrew tradition exaggerated when it claimed David could call up 1,300,000 able-bodied men who could use a sword (2 Samuel 24:9), for the total population of his kingdom must have been less than that, but it was true that power in the Iron Age meant the mass mobilization of common soldiers motivated by a common ethnic and religious purpose. In short, what we now mean by 'nationalism' entered history at this time. The social cohesiveness of primitive tribalism was reborn, but in social units much larger and more formidable than the primitive tribe.

THE KINGDOM OF DAVID AND SOLOMON *c.* 1000 BC

'And after this it came to pass that David smote the Philistines, and subdued them ... David smote also Hadadezer, the son of Rehob, king of Zobah ... Then David put garrisons in Syria of Damascus: and the Syrians became servants to David, and brought gifts. And the Lord preserved David whithersoever he went' (2 Samuel 8).

EGYPTIAN HIEROGLYPH		
SEMITIC PROTO SINAITIC 1600–1400 BC		
EARLY CANAANITE 1400–1300 BC		
CANAANITE c. 1200 BC		
EARLY PHOENICIAN 1100–1000 BC		
ARCHAIC GREEK FORMS 850–700 BC		
LATIN ALPHABET	A	Bb	N

THE DEVELOPMENT OF THE ALPHABET

The main Bronze Age scripts, Mesopotamian cuneiform and Egyptian hieroglyphic, were mixtures of ideograms and syllabic signs. After 1600 BC alphabetic scripts appeared in the Levant: Ugaritic, based on cuneiform, and traces of Sinaitic and Canaanite alphabets based on hieroglyphs. Canaanite evolved c. 1050 BC into the Phoenician alphabet, with its Aramaic and Hebrew variants. This table shows the evolution of the Roman letters A, B, and N, descended from hieroglyphs for ox, house, and snake.

One other Levantine development deserves mention. The Phoenician cities on the north coast, cut off from the interior and the Aramaeans by the massive ridge of Mount Lebanon, had survived the time of troubles by taking refuge behind stout fortifications. Some of these cities – Tyre, Sidon, Byblos – had been important ports even in the Bronze Age. The disorders of the new age brought perils but also opportunities, particularly in the expanding trade networks. While the Aramaeans were turning to camels and the desert, Phoenicians turned to ships and to the sea. They invested increasingly in maritime commerce, which they were soon transacting in a flexible alphabetic script like the Aramaic. As early as the eleventh century Phoenician ships began to explore the western seas in search of metals. In the process they probably invented naval warfare, or the early stages of it.

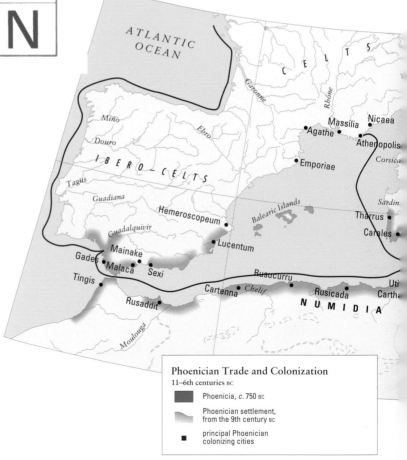

Phoenician Trade and Colonization
11–6th centuries BC

Phoenicia, c. 750 BC

Phoenician settlement, from the 9th century BC

■ principal Phoenician colonizing cities

Since armies began they had been moved about by water whenever possible. When the Egyptians fought in Palestine in the Bronze Age they usually sent their troops by sea; after the battle of Megiddo, Thutmose III always preferred this route for his northern campaigns. Piracy also was an ancient custom in the eastern Mediterranean. But none of this normally involved fighting at sea. Pirates rarely pursued merchants on the open sea because all ships carried both sails and oars and were therefore difficult to catch. (Pure sailing ships did not appear until the late sixth century BC.) The standard piratical procedure was doubtless that described in the *Odyssey*: the raiders beached their boats in the vicinity of a coastal town and then captured the place by land. Raiders could also blockade harbours by intercepting ships at the harbour mouth, and we hear of Levantine ports in the Bronze Age being blockaded in wartime, but as no ship could stay out to sea for very long this strategy required prior control of the coast so that the port could be besieged by land and sea simultaneously. In all these cases it would obviously have been desirable to cut off and board enemy ships at sea, but for the reason already mentioned this was difficult to do. The relief at Medinet Habu shows Egyptian ships intercepting the invading Philistines; but that was in the mouth of the Nile, and even there the feat must have required good timing.

PHOENICIAN TRADE AND COLONIZATION

Ezekiel's lament for Tyre: 'They of the house of Togarmah (Cimmerians?) traded in thy fairs with horses and horsemen and mules ... Arabia, and all the princes of Kedar, they occupied with thee in rams, and lambs, and goats ... These were thy merchants in all sorts of things, in blue clothes, and broidered work, and in chests of rich apparel, bound with cords, and made of cedar, among thy merchandise. The ships of Tarshish did sing of thee in thy market; and thou wast replenished, and made very glorious in the midst of the seas.' (Ezekiel 27)

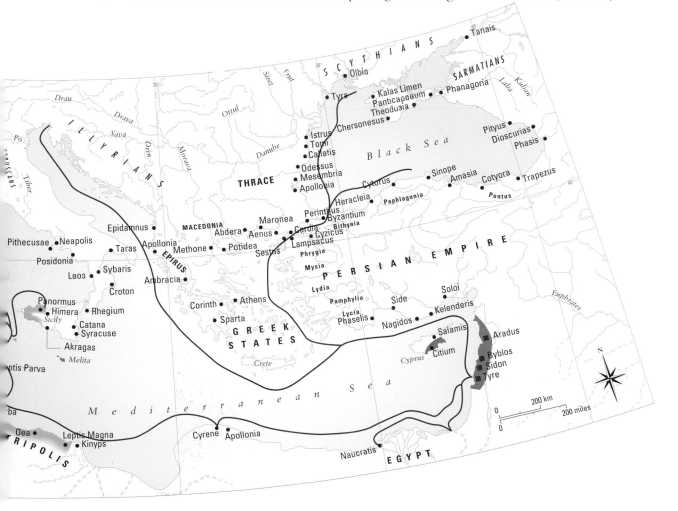

None of the ships in the Medinet Habu relief have rams, so this device did not exist around 1200 BC. But the evidence of Greek vase paintings shows that by around 800 BC the practice of fixing bronze rams to the prows of ships so that they could be used as weapons against other ships had become standard in the Mediterranean. Owing to the lack of pictorial records from the intervening centuries we cannot say with certainty when or where this device was invented, but it seems likely that it appeared within a century or so after 1200 BC, for much of the sacking of cities at that time was the work of coastal raiders, and there was urgent need for some method of coastal defence. It is unlikely to have been invented by the raiders, as it is not in the interest of pirates to sink their prey; but

War galley under sail, from a Greek vase painting c. 500 BC. These ships had twenty to fifty oars. The mast and sail were used for long-distance voyages but were left on shore when going into battle. Basically an open boat packed with rowers, the galley had little room for provisions and was usually beached every night.

after coastguards had rams, pirates of course acquired them too. The likeliest inventors of ramming were the Phoenicians, the leading seafarers of the time.

The standard warship of the early Iron Age was the penteconter, a 100-foot galley propelled by fifty oarsmen, twenty-five on each side; the word 'warship' is somewhat misleading, as there was no distinction between ships of war and merchant vessels, and the penteconters were equally useful for transporting trade goods (which were of small bulk at this time) and protecting them. In such ships the Phoenicians, followed by the Greeks, opened up the whole of the western Mediterranean to trade and colonization. Originally penteconters were built with only one bank of oars. The next step was the bireme, a shorter and more

EARLY WARSHIPS

The invention of the ram turned the galley into a self-propelled projectile which could destroy vessels by driving the ram into its hull. The ship might be decked or undecked, like this one. The oarsmen rowed from the gunwales. A fifty-oared galley had reached the practical size limit for a ship with one bank of oars, and after that the only way to increase power was to place rowers at different levels.

seaworthy vessel with its fifty oars arranged in two superimposed banks. This was in use by 700 BC; an Assyrian relief of that date shows the king of Tyre embarking in a bireme.

None of this amounted to much 'sea power' in the modern sense of that term; it was more like coastal power. We do not hear of sea battles before the seventh century, not even between Phoenician cities, and no big battles until the sixth, which suggests the fifty-oared galleys were for defensive purposes, to guard

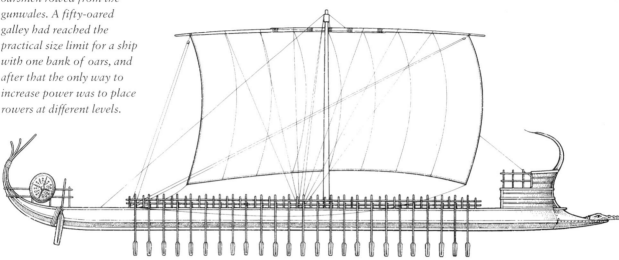

A relief from the palace of Sennacherib at Nineveh c. 700 BC is the earliest representation of a two-level galley or bireme. Rowers on the lower level work the oars through ports in the side. Those on the upper level row from the gunwales.

harbours and repel pirates. It is doubtful there were any naval tactics, which would require concerted action by a number of galleys. Real sea power had to await the invention of the trireme, a highly specialized ship with 170 oars in three banks, with more than three times the propulsive power of a penteconter, and useful for nothing but warfare. These expensive technological marvels were probably beyond the reach of a city state. They did not become common until the late sixth century, when the Persian Empire became a Mediterranean power, and the Persian king Cambyses, according to Herodotus, became the first man to aspire to command of the sea.

The Assyrian Empire

By the late tenth century the Aramaean expansion had reduced Assyria to its original heartland, a hundred-mile-long strip on the upper Tigris around the city of Assur. Then a series of energetic rulers began the rebuilding of the kingdom. Within a few decades they humbled the Aramaean tribes and restored Assyrian power to what it had been in the late Bronze Age, controlling the entire steppe between the Tigris and Euphrates. This effort must have required considerable military reorganization, perhaps borrowing Aramaean infantry tactics, but nothing is known about the organization of the Assyrian army until a much later period. What is certain is that in the early ninth century Assyria became ready to undertake the first great imperial experiment of the Iron Age.

The construction of the new empire came in two stages. The first, under Ashurnasirpal II (883–859 BC) and his son Shalmaneser III (858–824 BC), was a traditional empire of domination, like the earlier Mesopotamian empires. Almost every year the army marched out to collect tribute and acquire new client states, surrounding Assyria with a ring of vassals. They marched in every direction but concentrated on the west, where the Euphrates gave a direct route to Syria; this was a traditional avenue for Assyrian expansion, and interest in the west may have been sharpened by the need to control the Aramaeans. At first the tribute-collecting expeditions found it easy. Then resistance stiffened. In 853 BC the Syrian princes buried their quarrels and formed a united front against the Assyrians. The Aramaean king of Damascus led a coalition of twelve kings, including Ahab of Israel, to meet Shalmaneser at Qarqar. Shalmaneser claimed victory as usual:

> 14,000 of their warriors I slew with the sword. Like Adad, I rained destruction upon them. I scattered their corpses far and wide, and covered the face of the desolate plain with their widespreading armies … The plain was too small to let their bodies fall, the wide countryside was used up in burying them. With their bodies I spanned the Orontes as with a bridge.

Nevertheless Damascus was not taken, and Shalmaneser had to campaign in Syria for years to come. The total silence of the Bible about this major battle is

Assyrian archer, ninth century. Assyrian inscriptions and art became much more copious in the reign of Ashurnasirpal II. His fourteen campaigns extended Assyrian rule to and beyond the Euphrates and brought back much wealth, with which he built a grand new palace at Nimrud.

another reason to doubt it was an Assyrian victory, as the authors of the Books of Kings were not usually so reticent about the defeats of Ahab. But by 838 BC Shalmaneser had reached the Mediterranean and received tribute from many kingdoms, including Damascus and Israel.

In the last years of Shalmaneser a great revolt broke out in Assyria proper, perhaps caused by opposition of the Assyrian nobility to the rapid aggrandizement of the monarchy. The rebellion was eventually quelled but it nullified all the conquests of the last two reigns and for decades to come Assyria stagnated under a succession of weak kings. The first attempt to create an Iron Age empire had failed dismally. The old methods would no longer work. The empire of Ashurnasirpal and Shalmaneser had indeed been a Great Kingdom of the Bronze Age kind, a loose hegemonial structure consisting of a cordon of client states surrounding a core territory. Such an organization was difficult to sustain in a world when warfare was as much between peoples as between kings. Its collapse left Assyria ringed with danger: the traditional Aramaean enemies in the west were now supported by the rising kingdom of Urartu in the northern mountains, while Assyria itself was threatened with fragmentation owing to the increasing independence of the provincial governors.

The 'Black Obelisk' of Shalmaneser III, from Nimrud, shows defeated kings doing homage. On these two panels Jehu, King of Israel, prostrates himself before Shalmaneser. Israel and Damascus were the leaders of the anti-Assyrian coalition and Jehu's surrender symbolizes the southernmost extent of Shalmaneser's conquests.

Bronze door showing a fortress with soldiers, from the reign of Shalmaneser III. The revolts at the end of this reign were probably related to the problems usually ensuing from rapid expansion. For the next five reigns provincial governors seem to have been mostly on their own, but the core of the kingdom remained intact.

THE ASSYRIAN EMPIRE
824–625 BC

The documentation for this period is very rich by any previous standard: the royal annals, the great narrative reliefs from the palaces (examples of which are reproduced here), and over 2,000 letters on clay tablets.

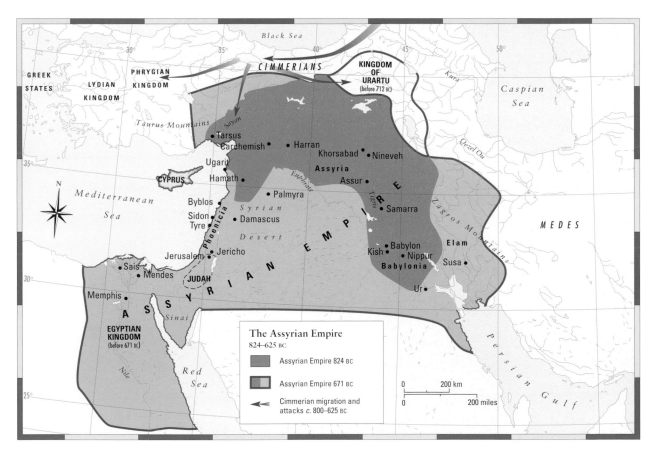

The Assyrian Empire
824–625 BC

Assyrian Empire 824 BC

Assyrian Empire 671 BC

◄── Cimmerian migration and attacks *c.* 800–625 BC

0   200 km
0   200 miles

Assyria was saved by one of these governors, who seized the throne in 744 BC and took the name Tiglath-Pileser III. He immediately began the reconquest of the lost territories and at the same time instituted a thorough reorganization. The foundations of the new empire were laid in the years 743–741 BC, when Tiglath-Pileser 'smashed like pots' a coalition of Syrian princes led by the king of Arpad, defeated an attempted intervention by the Urartians, and took the city of Arpad in a three-year siege. After this demonstration he turned south and received the homage of Damascus, Israel and the Phoenician cities. Then he turned his attentions eastwards: he pacified the Zagros range and penetrated farther into the Iranian plateau than any Mesopotamian had ever gone, reaching the neighbourhood of modern Tehran and setting up provinces in the land of the Medes; he invaded Urartu and laid siege to its capital on Lake Van. A second settlement of the Levant in 734–732 BC brought Damascus and most of Israel within the provincial system, while Judah and the Philistine cities were made vassals, extending the empire to the border of Egypt. A rump of the kingdom of Israel was allowed to survive as the puppet state of Samaria, but its king Hoshea rebelled at Tiglath-Pileser's death, whereupon his son Shalmaneser V took Samaria in a three-year siege and turned it into a province.

What Tiglath-Pileser III had created was not only the largest state in history thus far but the first centralized imperial state, and the model for all later

When Tiglath-Pileser III (744–727 BC) took the throne Assyria may have lost all its client states, though retaining control of north Mesopotamia. He extended the provincial system into Syria, established a cordon of firmly controlled clients over all the Levant, and finally declared himself king of Babylon.

empires. When the former client states were recovered, the nearer ones were usually turned into provinces under Assyrian governors, like the provinces of the Assyrian homeland. Beyond the provincialized area arose a cordon of new client states, which were now kept under a tight rein by Assyrian overseers. The provinces were subdivided until they numbered about eighty, to reduce the independence of the governors, who were required to report constantly to the

A relief from Tiglath-Pileser's palace at Nimrud: the Assyrian army besieges a city of the Medes, using a combination of scaling and ramming tactics. Auxiliary spearmen scale the walls with weapons in hand, covered by archers firing from behind high wicker shields. The ram is a light mobile structure on four wheels, with two poles ending in flat metal blades. The blades could be forced between the stones to prise them loose, causing a section of the wall to collapse. Before the walls the bodies of prisoners hang impaled on stakes.

king and subjected to frequent visits from his itinerant inspectors. The administration was served by history's first efficient postal service. By the end of Tiglath-Pileser's life, the whole of the Fertile Crescent north of Egypt, with adjacent parts of the Anatolian and Iranian highlands, containing several million people, had been brought within this system. He had also created or perfected the first great standing army, which will be studied more closely below.

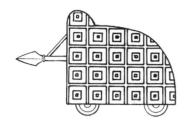

ASSYRIAN BATTERING
RAMS

*The upper figure is a
battering ram that appears
on a relief of Sargon II. The
lower figure is the ram from
the relief of Tiglath-Pileser
on the previous page. In the
eighth century Assyrian
rams became much lighter
than before (an earlier
model is shown on p. 196)
and were prefabricated so
that they could be
assembled on the spot.
They were deployed in
groups against certain
parts of a wall. The reliefs
of Sennacherib's siege of
Lachish (see p. 198) show
seven rams working
simultaneously.*

*The reliefs from the palace
of Ashurbanipal at Nineveh
are among the finest
examples of Assyrian
sculpture, especially the
famous scenes of the lion
hunt. Here Ashurbanipal
shoots his bow while his
spearmen fend off a
charging lion. The chariot is
one of the heavy four-man
vehicles typical of the
seventh century.*

After the short reign of Tiglath-Pileser's son Shalmaneser V (726–722 BC) his empire passed to the Sargonid house, which may have been another branch of the same family: Sargon II (722–705 BC), Sennacherib (704–681 BC), Esarhaddon (680–669 BC) and Ashurbanipal (668–627? BC), after whom several obscure kings or pretenders in a row presided over the sudden collapse. Thus the Assyrian Empire lasted hardly more than one hundred years, and to the end its boundaries remained essentially those established by Tiglath-Pileser. The Sargonids did little but round out the frontiers, and their only significant effort to expand them – the attempted conquest of Egypt by Esarhaddon – was never consummated. The empire seems to have reached its limits almost at the start, after which its resources were increasingly strained to hold on to what it had.

The Assyrian king was never deified like the Egyptian and many Babylonian rulers, but he was the viceroy and high priest of the god Assur, and hymns repeatedly reminded him to 'enlarge the territory of Assur'. He was told at his enthronement: 'Expand your land with your just sceptre.' The king was constantly addressed as if he were a universal sovereign: 'king of the four quarters of the world', who 'holds the rulers by their reins'. As Sennacherib put it:

Assur, the great mountain, has given me unrivalled kingship, and has magnified my weapon over all who sit on thrones. From the Upper Sea of the setting sun to the Lower Sea of the rising sun, all the kings of those regions he has caused to kneel at my feet so that they have drawn my yoke.

Yet it would be misleading to conclude from these theocratic formulas, which had been commonplaces of royal rhetoric since the Bronze Age, that the Assyrians believed in 'holy war'. In practice they assumed that all wars had to be justified by the traditional language of just warfare. Assur was a just god and his servant, the king, a just king; they went to war to strike down the wicked and protect the weak. The king was the 'light of all mankind', the 'shepherd of the world' under whom 'all the lands are dwelling in peace'. Temples to Assur were built in the provinces, but the Assyrians never made any attempt to force his cult upon conquered peoples. The images of the conquered gods were usually deported by the conqueror, a common practice in the ancient Middle East, but these images were not trophies; their deportation to Assyria was a sign of the defeated gods' submission to Assur, and the statues were usually repatriated after their worshippers had demonstrated their submissiveness and petitioned for the return of their deities.

It cannot be denied, however, that Assur was vindictive, even for a god. Assyrian kings routinely boasted in their inscriptions that they destroyed all cities they took and often claimed to have killed entire populations. These declarations served a deliberate public-relations purpose, as the punishments were meant as salutary warnings, and the most imaginative refinements of cruelty were reserved

for cities that resisted siege to the end. Only quotation can convey the flavour of these celebrations of pious terrorism. The following excerpts are from the annals of Ashurnasirpal:

> With battle and slaughter I stormed the city and captured it. 3,000 of their warriors I put to the sword; their spoils and their possessions, their cattle and sheep I carried off. Many captives from among them I burned with fire, and many I took as living captives. From some I cut off their hands and their fingers, and from others I cut off their noses, their ears, and their fingers (?), of many I put out the eyes. I made one pillar of the living, and another of heads, and I bound their heads to posts round

about the city. Their young men and maidens I burned in the fire, the city I destroyed, I devastated, I burned it with fire and consumed it ...

I took the city, and 800 of their fighting men I put to the sword, and cut off their heads. Multitudes I captured alive, and the rest of them I burned with fire, and carried off their heavy spoil. I formed a pillar of the living and of heads over against his city gate and 700 men I impaled on stakes over against their city gate. The city I destroyed, I devastated, and I turned it into a mound and ruin heap. Their young men and their maidens I burned in the fire.

Ashurnasirpal's son Shalmaneser III, not to be outdone, bragged that after

Siege scene from the 'Balawat Gates' of Shalmaneser III (mid ninth century) showing a six-wheeled battering ram. The poles extending from the rear may have been tongues to which oxen could be hitched. The battering pole appears to be fixed. The frieze also shows a lighter model with four wheels.

On the Balawat Gates tribute is collected and chariotry and infantry march. Shalmaneser had a pair of cedarwood doors 20 feet high made for his country palace at Balawat near Nimrud, each door covered with eight bronze bands embossed with these friezes which depict the king's campaigns during the first decade of his reign.

After crushing the Babylonian rebellion in 648 BC Ashurbanipal launched a desert campaign against the Arab nomads who had been raiding the frontier. On these reliefs from Nineveh, Arabs with simple bows, some on camels and some on foot, are easily overwhelmed by Assyrian cavalry and auxiliary foot.

taking one city he buried his captives alive under four pyramids of severed heads, surrounded by rings of stakes on which their countrymen were impaled.

Furthermore, the survivors were often deported to distant lands. This had been done before in the Middle East, but never on the astonishing scale initiated by Tiglath-Pileser III and followed by all his successors. Their inscriptions claim that between 750 and 620 BC, 4.5 million people were deported from defeated or rebellious territories and scattered all over the empire. Sennacherib claimed that he carried off 208,000 Babylonians at one sweep. Even if these figures are greatly inflated, there must have been massive redistribution of population. The most main purpose of this policy was to punish rebellion and to forestall it by breaking up disaffected communities, for usually an entire population or its élites were deported, many of them to disappear forever as ethnic groups. But the redistribution also served economic functions. Some deportees were conscripted into the army, but probably most were used as forced labour – rarely as outright slaves, for chattel slavery was never of great importance in Mesopotamia, but in various servile conditions, which often must have approximated slavery. They were moved mostly to regions ravaged by warfare or otherwise underpopulated, or to the burgeoning cities of the Assyrian homeland.

These policies may help to explain the premature demise of the empire. The system was by no means totally exploitative, or no more so than some later empires. The tribute, prisoners and other booty produced by the conquests were widely distributed. After the sack of Babylon, Sennacherib declared, 'I apportioned [prisoners of war] like sheep to all of my camp, my governors and the people of my large cities.' Ashurbanipal boasted that after a war against the Arabs he brought back so many camels that they sold for a shekel apiece in Nineveh and even tavern-keepers received camels and slaves in payment for drinks. The non-Assyrian population of the empire shared to some extent in its economic benefits. The Assyrian army was heavily recruited from non-Assyrian peoples. Even many of the deportees seem to have become prosperous and loyal Assyrian subjects in their new homes. Given enough time the Assyrians might have succeeded

German map of the site of Nineveh (AD 1900). The ruins of Nineveh lie across the Tigris from the modern city of Mosul. After Sennacherib rebuilt Nineveh c. 700 BC it was the main residence of the court. By the western wall Sennacherib built the huge 'Palace Without a Rival'. Ashurbanipal added the adjoining palace.

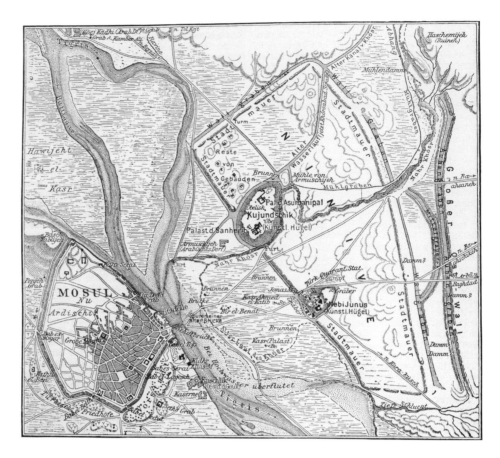

The restored walls of Nineveh. In the summer of 612 BC the city fell to the Babylonians and Medes after a three-month siege and was destroyed. The site was not reoccupied. The Greek commander Xenophon records in his memoirs that he saw the ruins in 401 BC but did not know the name of the city that had stood there.

in developing a diffused empire-wide governing élite, that did not have to rule by cruelty.

But there was not enough time. The basic problem with history's first empire was simply that it was the first. The system could not have been put together without an extraordinary amount of violence, and in the process too many implacable enemies were created. At the destruction of Nineveh in 612 BC the prophet Nahum claimed: 'All who hear the news of you clap their hands at your downfall. For who has not felt your unrelenting cruelty?' (Nahum 3:19). The successors of the Assyrians – the Babylonians, Medes and Persians – avoided this fate because they mostly took over the organization created by the Assyrians, whom they found an easy act to follow.

A few centuries later a somewhat parallel process took place at the other end of Asia. In northern China the transition from Bronze Age to Iron Age was once again accompanied by a shift from aristocratic chariot warfare to mass infantry tactics. The aggressive state of Ch'in specialized in the new art of war, conquered all its neighbours and created a centralized bureaucratic empire; but in the process it had recourse to such draconian measures that its dynasty was soon overthrown and its name became a byword for tyranny. It was replaced by the mild, stable, long-lasting regime of the Han Dynasty, which built upon the foundations laid by its violent predecessor, as the Persians took over the stained inheritance of Assyria.

THE ASSYRIAN ARMY

After the reforms of Tiglath-Pileser II the Assyrian military establishment consisted of several components. The most important of these was the *Sab Sharri* (Royal Army), the basic standing army, normally distributed about the empire under the command of the provincial governors. It included both ethnic Assyrians and auxiliaries recruited from the subject peoples. The chariotry, the cavalry and the heavy infantry were composed of native Assyrians, who in the ninth century had constituted practically the whole army. But after the expansion of the empire by Tiglath-Pileser the Assyrian troops were supplemented by large

ORGANIZATION OF THE ASSYRIAN AND PERSIAN ARMIES

Comparing these two structures we can see that the Assyrian and Persian armies were very similar in their organization. Although we do not know the strength of any Assyrian unit greater than the Fifty we do know that Assyrian Provincial Governors controlled a much smaller territory than the Persian Satraps. As a result the commands of the Provincial Governor, the Shaknu and the Rab Kisri would probably have been smaller than their Persian counterparts. The table suggests that the *Sha Qurbuti* were an élite unit of the *Kisir Sharruti*, an assumption drawn from the relationship between the Kinsmen and the Immortals in the Persian Army, although there is no evidence to confirm this.

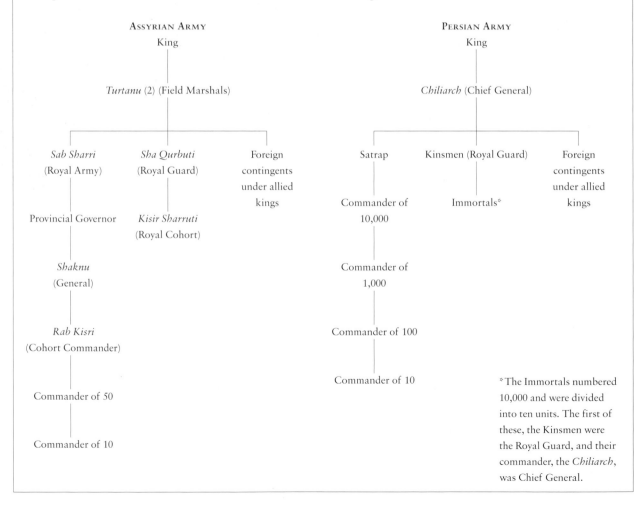

ASSYRIAN ARMY
King

Turtanu (2) (Field Marshals)

Sab Sharri (Royal Army) — *Sha Qurbuti* (Royal Guard) — Foreign contingents under allied kings

Provincial Governor — *Kisir Sharruti* (Royal Cohort)

Shaknu (General)

Rab Kisri (Cohort Commander)

Commander of 50

Commander of 10

PERSIAN ARMY
King

Chiliarch (Chief General)

Satrap — Kinsmen (Royal Guard) — Foreign contingents under allied kings

Commander of 10,000 — Immortals*

Commander of 1,000

Commander of 100

Commander of 10

*The Immortals numbered 10,000 and were divided into ten units. The first of these, the Kinsmen were the Royal Guard, and their commander, the *Chiliarch*, was Chief General.

numbers of auxiliary infantry units, both heavy and light, which tended to be drawn from certain warlike tribes like the Gurkhas of British India. The light infantry, usually unarmoured, included archers and slingers. Particularly valued were the archers, called Ituaeans because they were recruited from the Aramaean tribe of that name on the Tigris (though 'Ituaeans' was possibly shorthand for 'Ituaeans and other auxiliary archers'). The auxiliary spearmen were called Qurraeans; their origin is unknown, but their equipment suggests the Hittite cities of Syria. (Again, it is possible 'Qurraeans' meant 'Qurraeans and other auxiliary spearmen similarly armed'.) They were more lightly armoured than the

Assyrian infantry and wore a distinctive crested helmet instead of the pointed helmet of the Assyrians.

A document from Zamua gives us a precise numerical breakdown of the *Sab Sharri* troops under the command of a provincial governor in the reign of Sargon: 10 chariots, 97 cavalrymen, 80 Assyrian heavy infantrymen, 101 Assyrian staff, 440 Ituaean archers and 360 Qurraean spearmen; a total of 630 Assyrians (counting the grooms and other assistants who accompanied the horse troops) and 800 auxiliaries.

The Assyrians seem to have been recruited by the old method of landholding in exchange for military service; the auxiliaries may have been mercenaries. The basic unit was called a *kisru*, which may be translated 'cohort' or 'regiment,' but it is not known how many men it comprised.

There was also the *Kisir Sharruti* (Royal Cohort), an élite Assyrian force of unknown strength, perhaps created by Tiglath-Pileser; this seems to have been a

Many different types of soldier are portrayed in Assyrian art. This relief from Ashurbanipal's palace at Nineveh may depict soldiers of the royal bodyguard, the Sha Qurbuti *('soldiers close to the king'). Their equipment resembles that of the auxiliary infantry, except for the large shields.*

sort of Praetorian Guard under the direct command of the king. A still more élite unit formed the royal bodyguard, the *Sha Qurbuti*, which included cavalry, spearmen and archers. All these seem to have been equipped like the *Sab Sharri*.

Finally there were forces contributed by the client states on the frontiers. Some special foreign contingents, such as Israelite chariotry and Urartuan cavalry, are known to have served in the *Kisir Sharruti*, and perhaps also in the *Sab Sharri*. Others were called up in emergencies; for his main invasion of Egypt in 664 BC Ashurbanipal took with him, in addition to the regular army, foreign contingents collected from twenty-two princes of Syria and Palestine. These foreign troops, who are rarely depicted in art, used the equipment of their various traditions.

It has been estimated that the total forces available to Tiglath-Pileser and the Sargonids numbered half a million. We have seen that one provincial governor mustered 1,430 men, nor was this his entire command; we know that some governors sometimes had more than 20,000. Inscriptions sometimes speak of 100,000 troops mobilized for a battle. The history of ancient armies that are better documented – Persian, Greek, Roman – suggests we should reduce this number by half to get a maximum figure for an Assyrian field army, and halve it again to get the normal figure: perhaps a maximum force of 50,000 and an average one of 20,000. Armies larger than this were difficult to manage. Assyrian armies were not much larger than the biggest armies of the Bronze Age; the strict barriers that nature had placed on the size of armies would not be decisively broken until the nineteenth century AD. The real advances of the Assyrians lay in the little-known but clearly enormous logistical infrastructure that enabled huge armies to conduct long-distance campaigns the year round. A single statistic will suggest the magnitude of the supply problems: the archives of Nineveh reveal that

THE MAIN TYPES OF ASSYRIAN INFANTRY

Left, a Qurraean auxiliary spearman, identified by his round shield, crested helmet, and crossed chest straps. Centre, an Ituaean archer in kilt and headband. They were originally recruited from an Aramaean tribe called Itu'a. These two types are often encountered together in roughly equal numbers and must have fulfilled complementary functions. Right, an Assyrian heavy infantryman (kallapu) with conical iron helmet, corselet of metal scales, and huge shield.

QURRAEAN AUXILIARY
SPEARMAN

ITUAEAN AUXILIARY
ARCHER

ASSYRIAN HEAVY
INFANTRYMAN

the royal stables received an average of one hundred fresh horses every day, brought from all over the empire. There were five campaigns into Egypt within eleven years (673–663 BC), suggesting that logistical bases with horses, equipment and stores were stationed at intervals along that road and other well-travelled military routes. Armies carried rations with them, but the provincial governors and allied states were expected to provide food for men and horses, and it can be assumed this was high among their responsibilities. Armies also foraged in the countryside, especially during sieges, but the results must have been unreliable, as grain stores will have been brought inside the city before the siege commenced. The favoured campaigning season was still between the grain harvest (May–June) and the sowing (October), but campaigns in every month of the year are recorded, and in every type of terrain including mountain and desert. The king personally commanded whenever possible but there were two field marshals (*Turtanu*) and of course an elaborate but dimly viewed command structure lower down: commanders of cohorts (*Rab Kisri*), commanders of fifty, commanders of ten.

Cavalry were the great innovation of this army. Cavalry are first mentioned at the battle of Qarqar in 853 BC, where the Assyrians had 5,542 cavalrymen and 2,002 chariots, or about an equal number, since chariots at this date still carried two or three men. There was still some use for them, because in the ninth century the art of managing a stirrupless horse in battle had not been fully mastered: cavalrymen rode in pairs, one holding the reins of his companion and leaving him free to draw his composite bow, like the traditional partnership of chariot warrior and chariot driver, but without the chariot. Cavalry were cheaper, less vulnerable and more useful in rough country than chariotry, but not as yet superior in firepower. But the cavalry of Tiglath-Pileser and the Sargonids consisted of single horsemen, each rider armed with bow or spear or both. Assyrians had learned how to handle a composite bow on horseback. The chariot was thus obsolete by about 750 BC, for every rider now had as much firepower as a two-horse, two-man chariot.

The rise of genuine cavalry made possible genuine tactics, which is to say the art of combined arms, a variety of distinct services performing different roles in battle and doing so in co-operation. The Assyrian army certainly had such a tactical system, but it is not easy to reconstruct. We are well informed about military equipment, for the reliefs of the Assyrian palaces have left us the richest pictorial record of warfare before classical Greece, but not so well informed about how this weaponry was used on the battlefield. Assyrian annals, like all other ancient Middle Eastern records, are nearly devoid of useful battle descriptions. Assyrian sculpture, so dramatically effective in the portrayal of individual human and animal figures, never attained the Egyptian level of narrative realism. Neither infantry nor cavalry are ever shown in formation. There is no Assyrian battle that can be reconstructed in the way we can attempt to reconstruct the battle of Kadesh. Even the relief from Ashurbanipal's palace at Nineveh depicting the battle at the Ulai River in 653 BC, considered the finest large-scale composition in Assyrian art, is too broad and schematic, with too many chariots.

Nevertheless some things can be legitimately deduced from the tactics of the later Persian armies, which are believed to have been largely based on the Assyrian tradition, and are much better known to us through Greek sources. Persians put their infantry in the centre and their cavalry on the wings, which is such a common practice in all later warfare that we may assume the Assyrians did this too. The Persian army did not normally expect shock combat, but rather tried to break up enemy formations with missiles. The Medes, Persians and other Iranians who formed the core of their army were all lightly armoured bowmen, both infantry and cavalry. In battle the Persian infantry advanced and set up their large wicker shields as a hedge from behind which they fired their arrows; they closed in hand-to-hand combat with their short spears only when necessary. Their cavalry harassed the enemy before and during the battle by riding up and showering them with arrows and javelins, and after the enemy broke, cavalry were used in a mopping-up role.

Assyrian armies also consisted largely of missile arms and we suppose Assyrian tactics were similar, but there is reason to think that the Assyrians made rather more use of heavy infantry and hand-to-hand combat. The heavily armoured infantryman equipped with large shield and long spear, but no missile weapon, was the core of the native Assyrian army and figures prominently in Assyrian art. More than a century after Assyria fell Mesopotamian infantrymen of this type were still prominent in the Persian army. Herodotus (7:61–99) preserved the Persian army list of about 480 BC, which specifies the equipment borne by all the provincial contingents of the Persian Empire. Practically all are missile fighters – Iranian and Arabian archers, Anatolian and Thracian javelin-men. Only two regional contingents are equipped as heavy infantry with shield and spear: the Lydians of western Anatolia, who are armed like their neighbours the Greeks, and the 'Assyrians' (inhabitants of the Persian satrapy of Mesopotamia).

Assyrian armies were basically infantry armies. That was already clear in the ninth century, when an inscription of Shalmaneser mentions an army of 50,000 foot soldiers and 1,351 chariots. In the eighth century the ratio of foot to horse in the forces of the governor of Zamua was eight to one. We may assume that after some skirmishing by the cavalry the real battle was normally opened by the advance of the infantry. What was the infantry expected to do? In Assyrian art we often see an archer accompanied by a spearman who protects him with his shield, and on the Ulai River reliefs groups of archers and spearmen appear to be co-operating in some fashion. Perhaps they supported one another like the musketeers and pikemen of European infantry armies in the seventeenth century AD: the missile fighters opened the battle under the protection of the heavy infantry, and retreated behind them when it came to close combat. It may not be a coincidence that the governor of Zamua commanded precisely equal numbers of

spearmen and archers – 440 each. The Persians appear to have merged the Assyrian spearman and the Assyrian archer into a single all-purpose soldier, losing thereby the Assyrian capacity for shock combat. Assyrian battles, however, were probably won by archery. There would have been more scope for hand-to-hand fighting when Assyrians pursued an enemy already broken and fleeing, as portrayed on the Ulai River reliefs.

Cavalry doubtless operated in support of the infantry, which was always the role of cavalry in later armies: providing a screen for the advancing infantry, harassing the enemy with arrows, trying to outflank and encircle and break up their formations, pursuing them after they broke. They often carried spears as well, but as they had no stirrups and wielded their weapons with an overhand thrust they probably did not charge like medieval knights. Spears would have been most useful in riding down fleeing infantrymen, as on the Ulai River reliefs.

A long inscription by Sargon describing his great victory over Urartu in 714 BC provides one of the few semi-realistic narratives of an Assyrian battle. His army disorganized by the long march over the mountains, Sargon was unable to launch a conventional infantry assault, but won the battle by a single charge of his bodyguard cavalry, led by the king in his chariot. We notice that even at such close quarters the Assyrian horsemen appear to have shot arrows and thrown their spears.

> The exhausted armies of Assur, who had come this long distance and were tired and weary, who had crossed innumerable mighty mountains, whose ascent and descent were most difficult – their appearance became changed. I could not relieve their fatigue, nor give them water to quench their thirst, nor pitch my tent, nor strengthen the wall of the camp; I could not send my warriors ahead nor gather together my equipment (or army), what was right and left could not be brought to my side, I could not watch the rear. I was not afraid of his masses of troops, I despised his horses, I did not cast a glance at the multitude of his mail-clad warriors. With my single chariot and the horsemen who go at my side, who never leave me either in a hostile or a friendly

Detail from the reliefs depicting the battle on the Ulai River from the palace of Ashurbanipal at Nineveh. Assyrian infantry, consisting of spearmen and archers working in co-operation, push back the Elamites, who are mostly archers.

*On a relief from
Ashurbanipal's palace the
Assyrians storm an Elamite
city. Sappers undermine the
base of the wall while
Ituaean and Qurraean
auxiliaries mount the
ladders. If they could really
use their weapons while
climbing ladders, as pictured
here, they must have been
highly trained.*

region, the troop, the command of Sin-ahi-usur, I plunged into his midst like a swift javelin, I defeated him, I turned back his advance; I killed large numbers of his troops, the bodies of his warriors I cut down like millet, filling the mountain valleys with them. I made their blood run down the ravines and precipices like a river, dyeing plain, countryside, and highlands red like a royal robe. His warriors, the mainstay of his army, bearers of bow and lance, I slaughtered about his feet like lambs, I cut off their heads. His noblemen, counselors who stand before him, I shattered their arms in the battle; them and their horses I captured. 260 of his royal kin, who were his officers, governors and cavalry, I captured and broke down their resistance. Him I shut up in his crowded camp and cut down from under him his draft horses with arrow and javelin. To save his life he abandoned his chariot, mounted a mare and fled before his army.

In this battle only the king rode in a chariot, which was at that date on the verge of obsolescence. Because of their prestige, chariots continued in use long after cavalry, from the point of view of military effectiveness, should have replaced them. In battle reliefs chariots are frequently shown charging into the enemy. This was possible in Sargon's time because the chariot was still relatively light, carrying two or three men, and capable of operating as an adjunct of the cavalry, as described in Sargon's inscription. But in the seventh century the chariot became a much heavier vehicle, pulled by four horses and carrying four men – two archers, a shield-bearer and a driver. Their clumsiness and vulnerability to missiles makes it improbable that these vehicles were used in the charge. It is more likely that chariots had reverted to their original function and become mobile headquarters for transporting important men around the battlefield. The Assyrian king in battle was usually portrayed standing in an ornate command chariot under a tall parasol held by a eunuch. In the Persian army this was the only function of chariots, except for the scythed chariots (probably intended as

ASSYRIAN BATTERING RAM

Artist's reconstruction of a ninth-century battering ram of Ashurnasirpal, based on the engine shown in the relief on p. 18. It had a domed turret with embrasures through which arrows could be fired. The battering pole hung like a pendulum by a rope fixed to the turret roof. These huge engines did not last long. Later Assyrian rams were lighter and more portable.

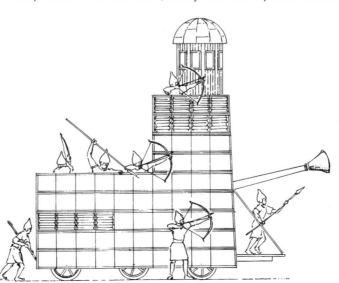

Continuation of the relief on pp. 194–5. The city has fallen and is plundered. Ancient cities lived in terror of sack. 'Every one that is found shall be thrust through ... Their children also shall be dashed to pieces before their eyes; their houses shall be spoiled, and their wives ravished.' (Isaiah 13:15–16)

psychological weapons) that played an ineffectual role in a few battles of the fourth century BC.

A pitched battle seems to have been an uncommon experience for the mature Assyrian army, because they were so good at it: most enemies sensibly avoided pitched battle with them, so most wars were won by sieges. Hence the most feared component of the Assyrian army was its siege-train, whose elaborate engines and techniques are prominently featured in Assyrian art. The Assyrian reputation for invincibility rested not only on the ability of their armies to go anywhere, but to overcome any possible defences once they arrived. Many sieges were very brief, proving that cities were regularly taken by storm. Esarhaddon took Memphis in half a day. The main innovation in siegecraft was the battering ram, which first appeared in the ninth century. It rendered obsolete the ancient and time-consuming tactic of building an earthen ramp to the top of a city wall and greatly expedited the business of taking cities by assault. When the Assyrians assaulted a city wall they often used three techniques simultaneously: battering rams, scaling ladders and sapping, all carried out under the protection of archers and slingers firing from siege towers as high as the wall. But there were also long sieges; it took three years for Tiglath-Pileser to take Arpad, two years for Ashurbanipal to take Babylon. In long sieges cities fell from starvation. An inscription of Ashurbanipal reports with satisfaction that the Babylonians ate one another during the siege of 648 BC. At the siege of Jerusalem Sennacherib's officer, taunting the Jews on the city wall, promised them they were doomed to 'eat their own dung, and drink their own piss' (2 Kings 18:27).

Relief from Nineveh: the siege of Lachish in Judah by Sennacherib in 701. Ramps of earth and timber have been thrown up against the wall and siege engines are being pushed up the ramps, protected by ranks of archers and slingers. Lachish fell but the siege of Jerusalem was broken off, according to the Bible by divine deliverance.

ASSYRIA'S ENEMIES

Assyria's problems were always complicated by a lack of defensible frontiers. The empire was vulnerable on three sides, of which the south-west frontier was actually the most secure, in spite of the recurrent efforts of Egypt (under a Nubian dynasty after 750 BC) to incite rebellion among the cities of Palestine. The revolt of Judah in about 701 BC was crushed by Sennacherib, after a siege of Jerusalem famous in Hebrew history. The revolt of Sidon in 677 BC ended in its destruction by Esarhaddon, and prompted him to round off the south-western frontier by conquering Egypt, which he did with deceptive ease in 671 BC. But none of the frontiers could be rounded off easily. Egypt never remained conquered, though Ashurbanipal invaded it twice (in 666 and 664 BC), and soon after he abandoned the effort, granting de facto recognition to the native Saite dynasty.

The south-east frontier was more vexing. The Assyrians were never able effectively to rule the ancient civilization of Babylonia, the shrines and traditions of which even the most powerful Assyrian kings were compelled to treat with reverence. Babylonia could be treated neither like a province nor like a client state; neither could it be absorbed. The task was further complicated by the ethnic heterogeneity of the land. The Akkadian population of the old cities was relatively submissive, but the south (the ancient Sumer) had been settled by a collection of restive tribes called the Chaldeans, and the desert by nomadic Aramaeans who were even harder to control. In addition, the neighbouring kingdom of Elam was always ready to support rebellion by any of these.

Various solutions were attempted. Tiglath-Pileser at first tried to rule the south through native Babylonian kings. These puppets could not manage the Aramaeans, so in the last year of his life Tiglath-Pileser himself took the title King of Babylon, as did his son Shalmaneser after him. But as soon as Shalmaneser died a Chaldean prince from the Gulf, named Merodach-Baladan (to use the biblical spelling of his name, which in Akkadian was Mardukapaliddina), claimed the throne of Babylon with Elamite support. The inscriptions of Sargon claimed a great victory over the Babylonians and Elamites at Der in 720 BC; this is unconvincing, as Merodach-Baladan is known from Babylonian inscriptions to have ruled securely in Babylon for the next decade. In 710 BC he was finally driven to Elam, and Sargon sat on the Babylonian throne for the last years of his life. Upon his death Merodach-Baladan promptly retook Babylon with Elamite troops. Sennacherib drove them out, but for years Merodach-Baladan continued the resistance from the impenetrable swamps at the head of the Gulf. In 689 BC Sennacherib finally vented his frustration by destroying Babylon, the holy city of Mesopotamia, and carrying off the statue of Marduk to Assyria. This was felt to be such a sacrilege that when Sennacherib was murdered by one of his sons in 681 BC, his younger son and successor, Esarhaddon, atoned by returning the statue of Marduk and rebuilding Babylon in grand style.

Esarhaddon tried to unite the two kingdoms by making two of his sons kings of Assyria and Babylonia respectively, but this solution did not work either; the king of Babylonia, who found himself treated more like a provincial governor, rebelled against his brother Ashurbanipal, which made it impossible for Ashurbanipal to recover Egypt. Ashurbanipal may then have taken the Babylonian throne himself. He tried to pacify the south-eastern frontier by undertaking the total destruction of Elam, the perennial support of anti-Assyrian elements in Babylonia. By 639 BC he was able to declare that Elam had been turned into 'a pasture for wild asses'. It was the last important Assyrian victory, and a fruitless one. About a decade later Babylonia was once again effectively independent under a Chaldean king, who was to watch Nineveh burn. Despite the massive deportations of its people, Babylonia had been growing in wealth and population, and the long and ultimately successful resistance led by Merodach-Baladan suggests that in spite of its ethnic mixture the country had acquired a sense of political and perhaps even national unity, forced upon it by the northern rulers.

The running sore of Babylon prevented the Assyrians from dealing effectively with the northern frontier, which turned out to be the most intractable of all, and the source of their final ruin. The heart of the empire lay on the fertile plains of northern Mesopotamia and Syria, which were vulnerable everywhere to the highlanders living in the great arc of mountains stretching from the Zagros to the Taurus. Assyria tried to intimidate these mountaineers by frequent raids, which only encouraged them to coalesce into increasingly formidable chiefdoms. In the eighth century there arose on the Anatolian plateau a powerful Phrygian kingdom (called Mushki in Assyrian records), occupying roughly the same territory as the old Hittite state. Its king Midas, whose wealth became a subject of Greek fairytale, was willing to spend much of it to cause trouble for the Assyrians in Syria. An even more dangerous neighbour was the kingdom of Urartu, straddling the ranges due north of Assyria proper, whose rugged terrain made it practically unconquerable. The Assyrians waged repeated campaigns against these northern kingdoms, but did not try to occupy them. Assyrian warfare relied heavily on siegecraft and the Assyrian imperial system was geared to ruling dense urban populations; the Assyrian reaction to a polity like the Urartian was to destroy it. Sargon in fact managed to severely reduce both Phrygians and Urartians. But that let in a more dangerous enemy.

Sometime in the early Iron Age the Aryan horse nomads in the north had mastered the art of using a composite bow on horseback, which was more difficult than shooting one from a chariot. They appear in Middle Eastern records for the first time in the reign of Sargon. In about 710 BC a mysterious people called the Cimmerians, who according to Herodotus had come originally from the Pontic steppe, inflicted a shattering defeat upon Urartu, which was never again to be a major power. Sargon was killed on the northern frontier in 704 BC, probably in battle with the Cimmerians. Soon after, the Cimmerians destroyed the Phrygian kingdom; King Midas is said to have killed himself by drinking bulls' blood. After this time the Assyrians seem to have given up Anatolia, which the Cimmerians completely overran. For a time they were resisted by Gyges, king of Lydia, an Assyrian ally, but about 650 BC the Cimmerians sacked his capital of Sardis and then harassed the Greek cities of Ionia. Another horde had turned eastward and invaded the Assyrian plain, where Esarhaddon claimed a victory over a Cimmerian king in 679 BC. The Cimmerians may have been the first people to realize the possibilities of cavalry; the first true nomad raiders, precursors of Attila and Genghis Khan. It may have been no coincidence that the Assyrian army learned the skills of horse archery at about the same time it made their acquaintance.

The surviving Assyrian oracle texts, which record royal attempts to discern the future, are largely concerned with the activities of the unpredictable riders of the north, whom Mesopotamian scribes had difficulty telling apart. Babylonians used the same word for Cimmerian and Scythian; but Assyrians distinguished a separate group of formidable horse archers called Scythians, who were said to have followed the Cimmerians from the Pontic steppe. Modern historians also find the identities and movements of the horse peoples a great puzzle. In their wanderings the tribal groups will have split and merged, and the 'kings' with whom Assyrians made war and alliance may be better described as temporary chiefs of certain bands.

The Scythians are particularly obscure because their ascendancy coincided

Assyrian soldiers with slings from Ashurbanipal's palace at Nineveh. Ethnic Assyrians, identified by their conical helmets, made up the heavy infantry and horse troops but could also serve as missile fighters, especially at sieges. Recent excavations at Nineveh have found the bones of defenders who fell in the siege of 612 BC.

Gold vessel from the Scythian royal tomb at Kul Oba, Russia, sixth–fourth centuries BC. After their defeat by the Medes the Middle Eastern Scythians rejoined their cousins on the Russian steppes. This warrior, wearing the typical Scythian trousers, boots, and hood, is stringing his composite bow by bracing it behind his knee.

with the failure of Assyrian historical records. Herodotus relayed a curious tradition that the Scythians had 'ruled over Asia' for twenty-eight years, during which time they had plundered the Assyrian empire at will and were bought off from invading Egypt by the Saite pharaoh Psammetichus, which would have been in Ashurbanipal's reign. For the reason given below, we suppose the period of Scythian dominance was approximately 653–625 BC, occupying most of Ashurbanipal's reign, and the tradition reflects the fact that by this time the whole of Assyria's northern frontier had crumbled.

But the most serious threat to Assyria came from a more civilized group of Aryans who had long been established on the western Iranian plateau. Their leading tribes were called the Medes and the Persians. Though they had retained their skills at horsemanship and archery, they had learned the benefits of ruling

agricultural peoples instead of raiding them; some Mede chiefs had become Assyrian subjects or vassals. For a long time they were dominated by the Scythians. But about 625 BC Uvakhshastra (called Cyaxares by the Greeks) united all the Medes into a kingdom with its capital at Ecbatana. Herodotus says Cyaxares organized an army consisting of cavalry, archers and spearmen: that is, he created an infantry of the Assyrian type out of the peasantry of Iran, and added this to his mounted horde, or what portion of it he could master. According to Herodotus he got the Scythian chiefs drunk at a banquet and murdered them. Probably he disposed of many in a similar fashion, but he probably also absorbed many Scythians and Cimmerians (who by this time were being pushed out of Anatolia by the resurgent Lydian kingdom) into his new federation; and the remaining Aryan nomads eventually wandered back to the European steppes, all of whose people were later called 'Scythians' by the Greeks.

The consolidation of the Median kingdom meant the doom of Assyria, which in 625 BC was already being torn apart by the gravest succession crisis in the history of the empire. As the annals of Ashurbanipal ended abruptly in 639 BC, after his conquest of Elam, the final collapse cannot be traced in detail. Ashurbanipal may have been forced to abdicate some years before his death in 627 BC. Certainly there was a civil war between two of his sons, and at some point the chief eunuch also claimed the throne. In 626 BC Babylonia saw its opportunity and declared its independence under a Chaldean dynasty. In 625 BC the Assyrian homeland was invaded by Babylonians from the south and Medes from the north. In 612 BC Nineveh fell to the allied army after a three-month siege and, as a Babylonian scribe wrote, was 'turned into a ruin heap'; and the Assyrian empire also, although a last Assyrian king, who may or may not have been a legitimate Sargonid, held out at Harran until 608 BC. It had been the most complex political structure that mankind had so far produced. The contrast between its unprecedented grandeur and its spectacular crash evoked wonderment in antiquity, and still does.

Babylonians, Medes and Persians

Nablopolassar, the Babylonian king who destroyed Nineveh, did not intend any great change in the order of the world. He wanted the Mesopotamian world empire to continue; he merely wanted it run from Babylon and not Nineveh. The northern territories, which Assyria had found impossible to control anyway, were left to the Medes. But the Babylonians were left in full possession of Assyria, which the Medes did not dispute apart from taking some border territory, and bent their efforts to the subjugation of the Levant, which was also coveted by the Egyptians. In 609 BC, when Assyria was tottering to its fall, the pharaoh Necho II moved to recover Egypt's ancient empire. He was resisted by Josiah, king of Judah, who was then sponsoring a national religious revival aimed at restoring (or more likely enforcing for the first time) the exclusive worship of Yahweh. The

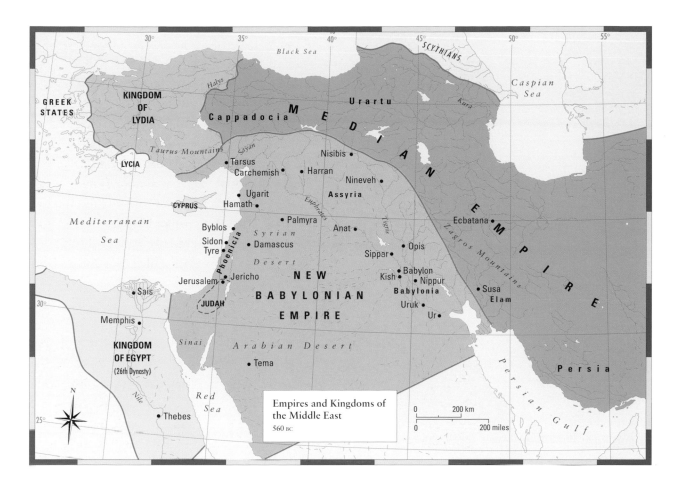

Empires and Kingdoms of
the Middle East
560 BC

0   200 km

0   200 miles

Egyptians defeated and killed Josiah at the old battleground of Megiddo, and then occupied Palestine and Syria all the way to the Euphrates. The new Egyptian empire lasted just a few years. In 605 BC, at Carchemish on the Euphrates, the Egyptian army, which included some Greek mercenaries, fought a bloody battle with the Babylonian crown prince Nebuchadrezzar and was annihilated. A few months later his father Nablopolassar died and Nebuchadrezzar inherited an empire almost as extensive as that of Assyria at its height, including the entire Levant as far north as the Taurus.

He also inherited the problems that had plagued Assyria in the Levant, including the meddling of the Egyptians and the recalcitrance of the Jews. Much of Nebuchadrezzar's reign (605–562 BC) was spent on the Mediterranean coast, campaigning against Egypt and putting down Egyptian-inspired rebellions. In 597 BC Judah revolted and Jerusalem was besieged and taken. Ten years later Judah led a coalition of Palestinian and Phoenician cities in a more dangerous rising. In 587 BC, after a siege of eighteen months, Jerusalem was sacked, the Temple of Yahweh destroyed, Judah turned into a province, and the Jewish leadership deported to Babylonia. In 571 BC Tyre was taken after a siege (perhaps not a continuous one) that is supposed to have lasted thirteen years and its king replaced with one more accommodating.

EMPIRES AND KINGDOMS
OF THE MIDDLE EAST
560 BC

The Babylonians have inherited the Assyrian Empire. Egypt is enjoying a period of stability and prosperity under the Saite dynasty. The Medes exercise some kind of rule over an immense territory but its nature is obscure; it may have been a very loose confederacy. In 585 a treaty between Medes and Lydians divided Anatolia between them at the Halys. West of that river the Lydian kingdom dominates Anatolia and will shortly take over the Greek city states of Ionia.

EMPIRE OF CYRUS THE GREAT C. 520 BC

Cyrus divided his empire into large provinces called 'satrapies'. After Darius's reorganization there were some twenty of these. Cyrus turned the former Babylonian Empire into a single satrapy called Athura (Assyria). Later the Levant was made a separate satrapy called Abr Nahir (Beyond the River).

One product of the reform of Judaism by Josiah was the doctrine of holy war (Deuteronomy 20), attributed to Moses, which commanded Israel to kill or enslave nonbelievers. This gave rise to the myth that the early Hebrews waged wars of extermination against the Canaanites. Here Joshua takes Jericho (from a medieval illustrated Bible).

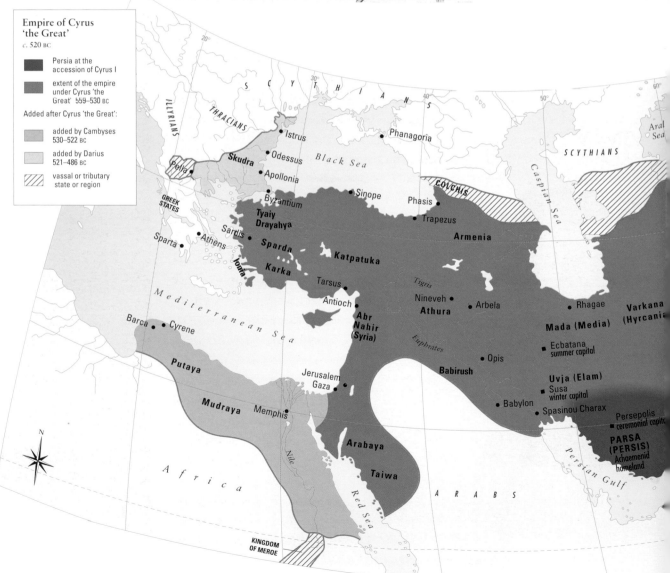

Empire of Cyrus 'the Great'
c. 520 BC

- Persia at the accession of Cyrus I
- extent of the empire under Cyrus 'the Great' 559–530 BC

Added after Cyrus 'the Great':
- added by Cambyses 530–522 BC
- added by Darius 521–486 BC
- vassal or tributary state or region

Little is known of the army of the neo-Babylonian Empire; it seems to have been modelled on the Assyrian military, but it also included Greek mercenaries. It was a more manageable empire than the Assyrian, but this was mostly because the Babylonians did not have to worry about the northern peoples, who had been subjugated by their allies the Medes. The splendours of Nebuchadrezzar's reign were deceptive, for his security depended upon maintaining good relations with the Median kingdom. He was also unlucky in his heirs, and the neo-Babylonian Empire did not long survive him. His line became extinct after three brief reigns and the throne passed to the pious and ineffectual Nabonidus (556–539 BC), who was interested mostly in promoting the cult of Sin the moon goddess, and who for unexplained reasons passed most of his reign in Arabia.

But in any case the world had grown too large to be governed from Mesopotamia any longer. Later the Greek sophists thought the succession of world empires had included Assyria, Media and Persia, but Babylonia did not make it into the list. The future lay with the Median kingdom. Cyaxares had tamed the horse peoples and absorbed them into an empire larger than the Babylonian, stretching from Iran to Anatolia. It was a loose federation rather than a centralized empire, as suggested by title 'King of Kings' adopted by Cyaxares and by many rulers of Iran after him. But it had a formidable army, both horse and foot, and potentially enormous manpower resources, and needed only a leader. One soon appeared. In 550 BC the Median king was overthrown by one of his principal vassals, Cyrus, king of the Persians. Cyrus then expanded his realm in both directions: in the west he overthrew the Lydian kingdom and took all of Anatolia, including the Greek cities; in the east he subjugated the whole Iranian plateau and extended his rule far into Central Asia. Within ten years he had built up by far the largest empire ever known, stretching three thousand miles from the Aegean Sea to the Indus River. The Babylonians read the handwriting on the wall and in 539 BC they opened their gates to Cyrus the Great.

Frieze from the palace at Susa, fifth century. This is probably an Immortal, a member of the royal infantry corps of 10,000 recruited from Persians, Medes, and Elamites. (See table on p. 186.) Persian infantry carried spears but were primarily archers.

Procession of court dignitaries on a staircase in the palace at Persepolis. Persian official art avoided the Assyrian celebration of barbarity. The Achaemenids achieved a stable regime that united the Middle East for 200 years, ruling through local élites and using Aramaic as the administrative language.

CONCLUSION

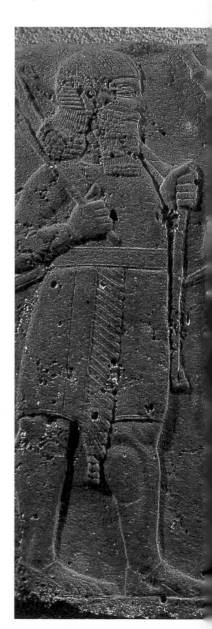

THE THESIS DEVELOPED in the last three chapters of this volume can be briefly summarized as follows. Three stages in the evolution of state-level warfare have been traced; these may be described in capsule form as the warfare of siege, of chariot and of infantry. Each of these military systems was associated with a certain type of political and social structure: the city state, the 'great kingdom' and the centralized empire.

It has been argued here that the first stage, appearing in Sumer in about 3000 BC, was essentially siege warfare. As soon as city states became capable of offensive warfare this opportunity was blocked by the rise of massive fortifications, producing a centuries-long stalemate in which only limited wars for limited objectives were feasible between city states. The stalemate was broken by the appearance about 2350 BC of the first of the great kingdoms, the Akkadian Empire, which commanded the manpower resources to take cities by storm. The new art of war, in co-operation with environmental stresses, seems to have spread destruction over the civilized world.

The next stage was initiated by the introduction of horsed chariotry in about 1700 BC, which made possible offensive warfare between states, and caused great kingdoms to rise across the Middle East. But the wars of the great kingdoms remained limited by the small size of their élite forces, so that decisive pitched battles were uncommon. This period ended in about 1200 BC in a second general crisis, this time it seems of a purely military nature, which again resulted in a general decline of civilization.

The third breakthrough came after 1000 BC with the rise of mass infantry formations supported by cavalry, dramatically increasing the scale and frequency of warfare and giving rise to centralized, bureaucratic multi-states that could command unprecedented resources. The organizational capacities of armies and the effectiveness of weaponry reached levels not significantly surpassed until modern times.

Soldiers march on the gate of Tiglath-Pileser's palace. 'Thy crowned are as the locusts, and thy captains as the great grasshoppers, which camp in the hedges in the cold day, but when the sun ariseth they flee away, and their place is not known where they are. Thy shepherds slumber, O king of Assyria: thy nobles shall dwell in the dust: thy people is scattered upon the mountains, and no man gathereth them.' (Nahum 3:17–18)

Offensive wars now became endemic and pitched battles (though still relying on missile rather than shock tactics) became common. Unlike the first two systems, this one did not end in a general crisis and collapse. Empires rose and fell but they were succeeded by larger empires. In an important sense, this stage is still going on. It was only in the early Iron Age that Clausewitzian warfare as we know it became a routine activity of states.

There have been many military breakthroughs since, as described in the other volumes of this series; some of these brought with them political and social developments of major importance, such as the development of infantry shock tactics by the ancient Greeks, and the gunpowder revolution of early modern Europe. But perhaps no developments in the history of warfare have been so fundamental and formative as the rise of the first armies.

APPENDIX

LANGUAGES OF THE ANCIENT MIDDLE EAST

Two hundred years ago no one could read any ancient Middle Eastern language except Hebrew and Greek. Since then about fifteen literary languages written in half a dozen different scripts have been recovered, and without doubt many important discoveries are still to come.

SUMERIAN

Sumerian, the first written language, is unrelated to any other known language. The first examples of its pictographic cuneiform script appeared late in the fourth millennium BC. Sumerian had its final flowering under the Third Dynasty of Ur (twenty-first century BC) when it was the official language of Mesopotamia for the last time. By Hammurabi's time it was a dead language but it enjoyed the status of Latin in early modern Europe and was much used for literary purposes. It continued to be studied in schools and used in liturgy in Mesopotamia until the time of Christ.

AFRO-ASIATIC (HAMITO-SEMITIC)

Afro-Asiatic (Hamito-Semitic) was the major language family of the region, as it is today. It has four main branches, one of which, Berber (spoken by the Berber peoples of north Africa, called Libyans in antiquity), was not written; a second, Cushitic (spoken by the peoples of north-east Africa called Nubians in antiquity), achieved written form only in some Nubian inscriptions in Egyptian hieroglyphics from the first millennium BC. The two great subfamilies were **Egyptian** and **Semitic**.

Egyptian hieroglyphic writing appeared in tombs in the twenty-ninth century BC; a cursive version called hieratic was used for administrative purposes. Egyptian remained the language of the common people of Egypt far into the Middle Ages and survives today in the form of Coptic, the liturgical language of the Egyptian Christians. It has the longest continuously recorded history of any language.

Semitic languages at the dawn of history were already spoken widely over south-western Asia. They are divided into East, West, and South Semitic. The last group is today dominant because it includes Arabic, but it entered our period only in the Sabaean inscriptions of Yemen (Sheba of the Bible), written in the eighth century BC in an alphabet derived from the Canaanite.

East Semitic was spoken in Mesopotamia along with Sumerian from the earliest times; some of the first kings of Kish in the *Sumerian King List*, supposed to be the first dynasty after the Flood, had Semitic names. The first written Semitic language was **Akkadian**, official language of the dynasty that united Mesopotamia. Akkadian was always written in the cuneiform script adapted from Sumerian. Between 2300 and 2000 BC it is called Old Akkadian. In the second millennium it split into a southern dialect (**Babylonian**) and a northern dialect (**Assyrian**). The classical literary dialect was Old Babylonian (2000–1500 BC), language of Hammurabi's empire. By the end of the Assyrian empire Akkadian had been largely replaced by Aramaic as the common spoken language of Mesopotamia, but continued as the literary language until the Persian conquest, and did not die out until the first century AD or later.

The earliest evidences of **West Semitic** are 'Amorite' personal names from the third millennium. Its first known written form was **Eblaite**, which was not discovered until the 1970s; this was the language of the city state of Ebla in Syria, written in a cuneiform script by *c.* 2500 BC. Later West Semitic tongues diverged into Canaanite, on the coast, and Aramaic, in the interior. The earliest literate version of Canaanite so far discovered is **Ugaritic**, which produced the first known alphabet (a consonantal alphabet, with signs for consonants but not vowels), adapted from cuneiform script *c.* 1400 BC at Ugarit (modern Ras Shamra) on the Syrian coast. In the first millennium consonantal alphabets were developed for three Canaanite languages, **Phoenician**, **Hebrew**, and **Moabite** (the last known from a single inscription) and another for **Aramaic**. Aramaic had the greatest success, becoming the common language of the

Assyrian Empire and later the administrative language of the Persian Empire. Two dialects of Aramaic survive today: Syriac, the liturgical language of many Eastern Christians, and a language called 'Assyrian' spoken by some Christian communities. Hebrew, of course, never ceased to be a learned language and is now again a spoken one.

INDO-EUROPEAN

Indo-European, the most widespread linguistic family in the modern world, has many branches. The first to appear was the **Anatolian**, written in a cuneiform script from *c.* 1650 BC (later a 'hieroglyphic' script, not related to the Egyptian script, was developed). This group includes the so-called **Hittite** of central Anatolia, the official language of the Hittite kingdom (the dialect was actually called Nesite, but its discoverers gave it the biblical name), **Luwian** in south Anatolia, and **Palaic** in north-west Anatolia. The Anatolian languages are very different from all other Indo-European languages and there is intense controversy over whether they were indigenous to Anatolia. This is part of the larger controversy over the origins of the Indo-European family and the reasons behind its vast dispersal (see Further Reading). In the first millennium Anatolian languages, including **Lydian** and **Lycian** (descended from Luwian) were still spoken in western Anatolia, and were then written in alphabetic scripts derived from the Greek.

In India, **Aryan** or Indo-Iranic developed into Sanskrit by *c.* 1500 BC. The history of Aryans in the Middle East is murky. Some Aryan words were in use in the Late Bronze Age, and their significance is discussed in the text. In the first millennium the Medes and Persians certainly spoke Aryan dialects, and by the time of the Persian Empire **Old Persian** (ancestor of modern Persian) was written in cuneiform. The Cimmerians and Scythians are widely assumed to have spoken Aryan also, though the linguistic evidence is very scant.

Mycenaean or Achaean **Greek**, ancestral to classical and modern Greek, was by *c.* 1450 BC written in the Linear B script. This is a syllabary, a script in which each sign stands for a syllable. (The as yet undeciphered Linear A was the script of the unknown language of the pre-Greek Minoan civilization of Crete.) By the eighth century Greek was written in the first true alphabet, with signs for both vowels and consonants, and had diverged into Doric, Ionic, and other dialects.

Phrygian, a poorly known Indo-European language of central Anatolia, has left some inscriptions written about the sixth century BC in an alphabet derived from the Greek. The language has no clear relations though some have thought it ancestral to modern Armenian.

ELAMITE

Elamite, the language of the ancient civilization of Elam, was written almost as early as Sumerian, at first in its own pictographic script, and later in cuneiform. The Elamite language survived in south-western Iran into the Middle Ages. It has been thought to be related to the Dravidian languages of India, leading some linguists to speak of an **Elamo-Dravidian** family. If this is correct then it is plausible that the language of the Indus Valley civilization, whose script has never been deciphered, also belonged to this group.

CAUCASIAN(?)

Hurrian was spoken over a wide area in and around northern Mesopotamia; its original home is uncertain and so are its affinities; some have thought it related to the Caucasian languages (such as Georgian). It was written in a cuneiform script by *c.* 2300 BC. In the second millennium it exercised a wide cultural influence because it was the language of the powerful kingdom of Mitanni. In the first millennium the kingdom of Urartu wrote its inscriptions in a Hurrian dialect but it is unknown whether this was the language of the people; because of their location some have thought they more likely spoke a proto-Armenian.

Caucasian origins have also been suggested for the mysterious **Hattic**, which to judge from its name must have once been the common language of Hatti. Some liturgical texts have been preserved in the archives of the Hittite kingdom, by which time Hattic was probably already a dead language.

Little beyond personal names is known of the languages of the various peoples of the Zagros region who appear in Mesopotamian history from time to time, such as the Guti and the Kassites; the suggestion that they were related to Caucasian seems to have nothing in its favour except a not very close geographical propinquity.

THE WARRIOR KINGS

All dates are BC unless otherwise stated.

MESOPOTAMIA

SARGON (2371–2316)

Founder of the Akkadian or Sargonic empire, became the subject of much legend, from which it is difficult to extract an historical kernel. It has been proposed that the dates of his reign should be lowered to 2296–2240, which would mean his dynasty was still reigning in Akkad at the time of Ur-Nammu of Ur.

NARAM-SIN (2291–2255)

Sargon's grandson, first Mesopotamian god-king, was also the subject of many legends; he was sometimes incorrectly portrayed as the last ruler of Akkad, whom the gods cursed for destroying the temple of Enlil at Nippur. According to the *Sumerian King List* the Akkadian dynasty was followed by the rule of the barbarous Guti; but if the revised chronology is correct this could not have lasted long.

UR-NAMMU (2112–2095)

Founded the Third Dynasty of Ur, sometimes called the Neo-Sumerian empire. According to the *King List* the Gutian invaders were expelled by the king of Uruk, who was in turn replaced by Ur-Nammu of Ur. His dates should perhaps be lowered to 2047–2030. The history of his dynasty is little known. He was remembered for his building projects and his reign was relatively peaceful, but he died in battle.

SHULGI (2094–2047)

The son of Ur-Nammu and the greatest king of Ur III. Like Naram-Sin of Akkad, he took the title King of the Four Quarters and deified himself. He was a patron of learning, but almost constantly at war, and built a fortified wall between the Tigris and Euphrates to keep out barbarian invaders.

SHAMSHI-ADAD I (1813–1781)

An Amorite prince who became king of Assur and briefly united northern Mesopotamia. Later he was given a false genealogy and inserted into the *Assyrian King List*, so some scholars have called his realm the First Assyrian Empire; but there was nothing Assyrian about it and it is better described as the Upper Mesopotamian Kingdom. It was larger than the empire of Hammurabi which succeeded it but just as impermanent.

HAMMURABI (1792–1750)

The sixth ruler of an Amorite dynasty that had ruled the unimportant city of Babylon since 1894. By adroit diplomacy he briefly reunited Mesopotamia almost to its Sargonic boundaries. In *c.* 1760 he absorbed Larsa, then the major power in the south, and a few years later acquired Eshnunna, chief city of the north.

TIKULI-NINURTA I (1244–1208)

One of the most energetic kings of the Middle Assyrian Kingdom, as the Assyrian state is sometimes called after Ashur-uballit I took the title Great King of Assyria *c.* 1350. In alliance with Elam he captured Babylon and proclaimed himself King of Babylon. He was overthrown and killed by a revolt of his nobles. He became the subject of the only surviving Assyrian epic, and passed into the Bible as Nimrod, 'a mighty hunter before the Lord' (Genesis 10).

TIGLATH-PILESER I (1114–1076)

The last important Middle Assyrian ruler. In incessant campaigns he pushed back the Phrygians and Aramaeans, reached the Mediterranean and received tribute from Phoenician cities. He also inflicted heavy casualties on Middle Eastern wildlife, accounting for 10 bull elephants, 4 bull aurochs, 920 lions (120 on foot and the rest in his chariot), and a 'sea horse' in Mediterranean waters (some kind of cetacean?).

ASHURNASIRPAL II (883–859)

Is counted the founder of the 'Neo' Assyrian empire, but his conquests did not depart from earlier patterns of Assyrian control; he considered himself to be recovering lands that had belonged to the empire of Tiglath-Pileser I, and the conquered were considered Assyrian subjects who were in 'revolt'.

SHALMANESER III (858–824)

Son of Ashurnasirpal, completed the restoration of the old Assyrian empire and then permanently extended his conquests beyond the Euphrates. His empire in the Levant was overextended and his home base neglected, and in his last years his acquisitions were swept away during a revolt of the Assyrian nobles.

TIGLATH-PILESER III (744–727)

Usurped the throne but may have been of royal blood; such things are difficult to determine because Assyrians kept up the fiction that all their kings had belonged to a single dynasty since c. 1500. There is no need to recapitulate his achievements. He is considered the greatest of Assyrian rulers, creator of the centralized empire and army.

SARGON II (721–705)

Likewise may or may not have been a usurper. For the next century his descendants, sometimes called the Sargonids, ruled in unbroken succession. Major events in his constant wars were the indecisive battle at Der against Babylonians and Elamites, his defeat of Syro-Palestinian rebels at the old battleground of Qarqar, the first Assyrian victory over Egypt at Raphia, and his decisive victory over Urartu. He built a new capital at Dur-Sharrukin, 'Sargonsburg' (modern Khorsabad) but later kings preferred the traditional capitals of Nimrud and Nineveh. (Assyrian kings were buried in the ancient capital of Assur but did not normally live there.)

SENNACHERIB (704–681)

Son of Sargon, was occupied with revolts in the Levant, including a famous siege of Jerusalem, and in Babylonia, where he fought a major battle at Hallule and destroyed Babylon. He rebuilt Nineveh and made it the main capital of the empire. He was murdered by two of his sons.

ESARHADDON (680–669)

Younger son of Sennacherib, took over after a civil war against his brothers. He rebuilt Babylon, destroyed rebellious Sidon, and undertook the conquest of Egypt, driving the Nubian pharaoh Taharka back to Nubia. But two years later Taharka returned and retook Egypt, and Esarhaddon died on a second Egyptian campaign.

ASHURBANIPAL (668–627?)

Son of Esarhaddon, was occupied with the partly successful reconquest of Egypt, the successful suppression of the revolt of his brother the king of Babylon, and the successful annihilation of Elam; but the last decade of his reign, when the empire fell apart, is a mystery. His great library at Nineveh is a major source of our knowledge of Mesopotamian literature.

NEBUCHADREZZAR II (604–562)

The only great ruler of the Neo-Babylonian or Chaldean dynasty, rebuilt Babylon and was given credit for the Hanging Gardens and other architectural wonders. In foreign affairs he was occupied with wars against Egypt, one by-product of which was the destruction of Jerusalem.

HATTI

HATTUSILIS I (1650–1620)

Founded the Hittite 'Old Kingdom'. His dates are uncertain. King of Kussara, he made Hattusas his capital because of its impregnable position – his name means 'man of Hattusas' – united Hatti (central Anatolia), fought against Hurrians to the east and Luwians to the west, and made two expeditions across the Taurus to challenge Yamhad (Aleppo) for the mastery of Syria.

MURSILIS I (1620–1590)

Hattusilis' grandson, sacked Aleppo and destroyed the kingdom of Yamhad, then marched almost 1,000 miles to sack Babylon. The middle chronology puts this raid in 1595, but some would move it sixty years either way. On his return Mursilis was assassinated by his brother-in-law and his Syrian conquests did not last.

SUPPILULIUMAS I (1344–1322)

Restored Hittite power after a long decline and is considered founder of the 'New Kingdom' or 'Empire'. He destroyed the kingdom of Mitanni, sacking its capital Washukkani. He took from Egypt (then distracted by the religious reforms of the heretic pharaoh Akhenaten) the client states of Ugarit, Kadesh, and Amurru, and made his sons viceroys of Carchemish and Aleppo, thus establishing Hittite control over much of Syria.

MUTAWALLIS II (1295–1271)

Grandson of Suppiluliumas, reigned over the Hittite empire at its height. He defended Syria from the Nineteenth Dynasty pharaohs Seti I and Ramesses II, and at Kadesh in 1275 fought the greatest of all Hittite battles, making possible the permanent peace settlement his brother Hattusilis III made with Ramesses in 1259.

NEW KINGDOM – EGYPT

THUTMOSE III (1479–1425)

Greatest ruler of the Eighteenth Dynasty, was responsible for the Egyptian empire in the Levant, though his grandfather Thutmose I once conducted an expedition as far as the Euphrates. After the battle of Megiddo in his twenty-second year Thutmose III campaigned there almost annually, mostly in the north around Byblos. Some of these were punitive expeditions, others were displays of strength. In 1446 he marched all the way to Mitanni, pausing on the way to hunt elephants on the Orontes, and put up a stele on the banks of the Euphrates.

AMENHOTEP II (1427–1401)

Son of Thutmose III, was equally interested in the Asian empire and made several campaigns to punish 'rebels', establishing firm Egyptian control of the

coast north to Amurru and a looser sphere of influence north to Ugarit.

SETI I (1294–1279)

Second pharaoh of the Nineteenth Dynasty, waged several campaigns to restore Egyptian authority in Canaan. In the north he retook Amurru, fought a battle against Mutawallis the Hittite, and may have concluded a treaty with him. He commemorated his wars in many battle reliefs in Egyptian temples.

RAMESSES II (1279–1212)

Called the Great, was the son of Seti and resumed his program of imperial reconquest. In his fourth year he challenged Mutawallis by campaigning north to Amurru; in his fifth year came the standoff at Kadesh, after which Ramesses had to put down many revolts in Canaan, and eventually worked out a settlement with the Hittites. He left 138 known progeny, and self-glorifying monuments all over Egypt and Nubia. (He is the 'Ozymandias' of Shelley's poem.) His influence was such that the period of the Nineteenth and Twentieth Dynasties is sometimes called the 'Ramesside' age, for Ramesses II accounted all by himself for most of the Nineteenth Dynasty, and all but one of the ten pharaohs of the Twentieth Dynasty took the name 'Ramesses'.

RAMESSES III (1186–1155)

Second pharaoh of the Twentieth Dynasty, is remembered for the victories commemorated in his mortuary complex at Medinet Habu near Thebes. The inscriptions claim that in his fifth year (1182) he defeated Libyans who attacked the western Delta and killed 12,535 of them; in his eighth year (1179) he defeated Philistines and others attacking from the east on both land and sea. There is much controversy over the interpretation of these reliefs. Some show women and children travelling in oxcarts, which has been taken as evidence for a mass migration by 'Sea Peoples', but the reliefs have recently been reinterpreted as a representation of villagers fleeing from an Egyptian raid into Canaan, maybe in retaliation for the raid of 1179.

FURTHER READING

Ancient texts often contain gaps, and modern editors must supply the missing words. For ease in reading brackets indicating reconstructions have generally been omitted from the translations quoted in this volume, and some spellings slightly simplified; readers interested in these points should consult the original texts.

Most general military histories pay slight attention to anything before classical Greece. A notable exception is John Keegan, *A History of Warfare* (NY, 1993). The following books are interpretative surveys for the general reader covering warfare from the Paleolithic through the ancient Middle East: Arther Ferrill, *The Origins of War: From the Stone Age to Alexander the Great* (London, 1985); R. L. O'Connell, *Ride of the Second Horseman: The Birth and Death of War* (New York, 1995); and Doyne Dawson, *The Origins of Western Warfare: Militarism and Morality in the Ancient World* (Boulder, 1996). Sociological studies dealing with early warfare include Michael Mann, *The Sources of Social Power, Volume I: A History of Power from the Beginnings to A.D. 1700* (Cambridge, 1986) and Joseph Tainter, *The Collapse of Complex Societies* (Cambridge, 1988).

I have treated the origins of war in more depth in 'Evolutionary Theory and Group Selection: The Question of Warfare', *History and Theory*, Theme Issue 38 (The Return of Science: Evolutionary Ideas and History, 1999), pp. 79–100. On Darwinian psychology see *The Adapted Mind: Evolutionary Psychology and the Generation of Culture*, ed. J. H. Barkow, Leda Cosmides, and John Tooby (NY, 1992). On group selection, see Elliot Sober and D. S. Wilson, *Unto Others: The Evolution and Psychology of Unselfish Behavior* (Cambridge, Mass., 1998). Introductions to human evolution are numerous and quickly outdated, but Ian Tattersall, *Becoming Human: Evolution and Human Uniqueness* (NY, 1998) can be recommended to readers who want a current survey more sceptical of Darwinian psychology than the present author. See also the essays collected in *Sociobiology and Conflict: Evolutionary Perspectives on Competition, Cooperation, Violence, and Warfare*, ed. J. M. G. Van der Dennen and V. Falger (London, 1990). Different views on the primate connections of warfare can be found in *The Evolution of Human Behavior: Primate Models*, ed. W. G. Kinzey (NY, 1987); R. W. Wrangham and Dale Peterson, *Demonic Males: Apes and the Origins of Human Violence* (Boston, 1996); Craig Stanford, *The Hunting Apes: Meat Eating and the Origins of Human Behavior* (Princeton, 1999). On the cultural revolution, see *The Human Revolution: Behavioural and Biological Perspectives on the Origins of Modern Humans*, ed. Paul Mellars and Chris Stringer (Edinburgh, 1989). On Machiavellian intelligence, see Richard Byrne, *The Thinking Ape: Evolutionary Origins of Intelligence* (Oxford, 1995), and Stephen Mithen, *The Prehistory of the Mind: A Search for the Origins of Art, Religion, and Science* (London, 1996).

In the second chapter I make use of a study of New Guinea warfare by Joseph Soltis, Robert Boyd, and P. J. Richerson, 'Can Group-functional Behaviors Evolve by Cultural Group Selection? An Empirical Test', *Current Anthropology* 36 (1995), pp. 473–94; and a study of the causes of war by Carol and Melvin Ember, 'Resource Unpredictability, Mistrust, and War: A Cross-Cultural Study', *Journal of Conflict Resolution* 36 (1992), pp. 242–62. Readers interested in exploring anthropological models that offer alternatives to the Darwinian approach adopted here might consider the ecological school represented by Marvin Harris – I have quoted from his *Our Kind: Who We Are, Where We Came From, Where We Are Going* (NY, 1989) – and the skeptical approach of C. R. Hallpike, *The Principles of Social Evolution* (Oxford, 1986) - my quotation is from his commentary on the article by Soltis et al. in *Current Anthropology*. On primitive warfare see essays collected in *Warfare, Culture, and Environment*, ed. R. B. Ferguson (Orlando, 1984), and *The Anthropology of War*, ed. Jonathan Haas (Cambridge, 1990). Lawrence Keeley, *War Before Civilization: The Myth of the Peaceful Savage* (NY, 1996) is a useful study of archeological evidence but should be used with caution on historical and philosophical questions. On the origins of agriculture I have followed the interpretation of M. N. Cohen, *The Food Crisis in Prehistory: Overpopulation and the Origins of Agriculture* (New Haven, 1977). The circumscription thesis first appeared in Robert Carnciro, 'A Theory of the Origins of the State', *Science* 169 (1970), pp. 733–8.

On the ancient Middle East the most recent survey is Amélie Kuhrt, *The Ancient Near East c. 3000–300 BC*, 2 vols. (London, 1995), and the fullest is the latest edition of *The Cambridge Ancient History*, vols. I.2–III.2 (Cambridge, 1971–91). On warfare, Yigael Yadin, *The Art of War in Biblical Lands in the Light of Archaeological Discovery* (London, 1963), remains invaluable both for text and illustrations. Essays on many subjects including warfare will be found in *Civilizations of the Ancient Near East*, ed. J. M. Sasson, 4 vols. (NY, 1995). Michael Roaf, *Cultural Atlas of Mesopotamia and the Ancient Near East* (NY, 1990) is a convenient collection of maps and illustrations.

On Mesopotamia in the Early and Middle Bronze Age see J. N. Postgate, *Early Mesopotamia: Society and Economy at the Dawn of History* (NY, 1992), source of most of the translations quoted in the third chapter. For translations of and commentary on the Lagash inscriptions see J. S. Cooper, *Reconstructing History from Ancient Inscriptions: The Lagash-Umma Border Conflict* (Malibu, 1983). The Sargon inscription is from *Ancient Near Eastern Texts Related to the Old Testament*, ed. J. B. Pritchard, 3rd ed. (Princeton, 1969). For recent research on the Akkadian period see the papers collected in *Akkad: The First World Empire – Structure, Ideology, Traditions*, ed. Mario Liverani (Padua, 1993). Another recent collection of papers, *Third Millennium BC Climate Change and Old World Collapse*, ed. H. N. Dalfes, George Kukla, and Harvey Weiss (Berlin, 1997), addresses the problem of the end of the Early Bronze Age. On the Mari documents there is Sasson, *The Military Establishment at Mari* (Rome, 1969), source of the translation from Shamshi-Adad.

The beginning of chariot warfare in the High or Late Bronze Age is studied by Robert Drews, *The Coming of the Greeks: Indo-European Conquests in the Aegean and the Near East* (Princeton, 1988). Other theories about the dispersal of the Indo-European languages would place it at a much earlier date: see *Colin Renfrew, Archaeology and Language: The Puzzle of Indo-European Origins* (London, 1987), and J. P. Mallory, *In Search of the Indo-Europeans: Language, Archaeology, and Myth* (London, 1989). M. A. Littauer and J. H. Crouwel, *Wheeled Vehicles and Ridden Animals in the Ancient Near East* (Leiden, 1979) is indispensable for the history of chariots and cavalry. Mario Liverani, *Prestige and Interest: International Relations in the Near East 1600–1100 BC.* (Padua, 1990) is a mine of information about the High Bronze Age and the source of the translations in the fourth chapter, except for the inscriptions of Thutmose III and Ramesses III, which are from Pritchard, and those of Ramesses II, which are from Sir Alan Gardiner, *The Kadesh Inscriptions of Ramesses II* (Oxford, 1975). Papers collected in *The Crisis Years: From Beyond the Danube to the Tigris*, ed. W. A. Ward and M. S. Joukowsky (Dubuque, 1992) examine various aspects of the fall of Bronze Age civilization. The interpretation of Drews, *The End of the Bronze Age: Changes in Warfare and the Catastrophe c. 1200 BC.* (Princeton, 1993) is still controversial but in the view of the present author the most satisfactory explanation yet offered. For the Hittites there is now Trevor Bryce, *The Kingdom of the Hittites* (Oxford, 1998).

Lionel Casson, *Ships and Seafaring in Ancient Times* (Austin, 1994) is a well-illustrated summary of research by Casson and other scholars. See also H. T. Wallinga, *Ships and Sea-Power Before the Great Persian War* (Leiden, 1993).

H. W. F. Saggs, *The Might That Was Assyria* (London, 1984), is a general history. There is no book in English on Assyrian warfare: see Florence Malbran-Lablat, *L'armée et l'organisation militaire de l'Assyrie* (Paris, 1982); Walter Mayer, *Politik und Kriegskunst der Assyrer* (Münster, 1995); and for a translation of the Zamua document, Postgate, 'The Assyrian Army in Zamua', *Iraq* 62 (2000), pp. 89–108. Israel Eph'al, 'On Warfare and Military Control in the Ancient Near Eastern Empires: A Research Outline', in *History, Historiography, and Interpretation: Studies in Biblical and Cuneiform Literatures*, ed. H. Tadmor and M. Weinfeld (Jerusalem, 1984), pp. 88–106, is primarily concerned with Assyria. Aspects of Assyrian imperialism have been studied in Morton Cohen, *Imperialism and Religion: Assyria, Judah, and Israel in the Eighth and Seventh Centuries B.C.* (Missoula, 1974); *Power and Propaganda: A Symposium on Ancient Empires*, ed. M. T. Larsen (Copenhagen, 1979); Bustenay Oded, *Mass Deportations and Deportees in the Neo-Assyrian Empire* (Wiesbaden, 1979), source of the translations quoted on p. 182, and *War, Peace, and Empire: Justifications for War in Assyrian Royal Inscriptions* (Wiesbaden, 1992), source of the translation on p. 176). Other translations in the last chapter are drawn from *Ancient Records of Assyria and Babylonia*, ed. D. D. Luckenbill, 2 vols. (NY, 1927).

INDEX

Figures in *italic* refer to captions

PICTURE CREDITS

AKG Endpapers and pp. 14, 38, 39, 41, 43, 46, 49, 70–1, 76, 126–7, 133, 136, 139, 151, 154–5, 171, 172, 184, 206, 211; Werner Forman Archive pp. 6, 68, 69, 72, 101, 102–3, 109, 112, 142, 144, 156, 157, 158, 168, 170, 187, 192, 197, 198, 202; Corbis / Charles & Josette Lenars p. 12, Archivo Iconografico 22, 53, Bettmann 23, 24, 73, Penny Tweedie 26, 44–5, David Lees 77, Chris Hellier 121; Art Archive pp. 15, 67, 74, 81, 82, 84–5, 92, 93, 96, 108, 117, 118, 125, 128, 130, 137, 143, 146–7, 177, 183, 191, 194–5, 203, 207, 208–9; British Museum pp. 18–19, 80, 83, 86, 106–7, 115, 160, 174–5, 178–9, 180–1; BBC Natural History Unit pp. 20, 27, 28–9, 30–1; Oxford Scientific Films pp. 33, 34, 35, 51, 58–9; Natural History Museum pp. 37, 40, 42; Ancient Art & Architecture Collection pp. 54-5, 166–7, 173, 185; Hutchison Library pp. 56, 61; Mary Evans Picture Library pp. 62, 64–5.

Drawings on the title page and on pages 54, 83, 86, 94, 97, 100, 101, 114, 120, 122, 123, 128, 164, 168, 176, 188 and 196 are by Peter Smith and Malcolm Swanston of Arcadia Editions Ltd

ENDPAPER: *Detail from the relief of the sea battle at Medinet Habu. The* Sherden *are distinguished by their horned helmets, long swords, and small round shields. Doubtless many came from Sardinia, but the word* Sherden *may have been used for any foreign mercenary serving as a skirmisher or chariot-runner. They play a prominent part in the reliefs of the battle of Kadesh, where they act as the pharoah's bodyguard, and in the sea battle of 1179 they are shown fighting on both sides.*